Praise for Cezary Łazarewicz

"*Leave No Trace* is a book that shuns sentimentalism and martyrdom, yet it is hard to forget the volumes of despair (victims), cynicism (tormentors), and injustice contained in it. It draws you in completely like some perverse, cruel detective story. *Leave No Trace* is simply a knock-out."
—*CULTURE.pl*

"[*Nothing personal. The Case of Janusz Waluś*] is a book that won't let you rest. You can swallow it in one evening, but it's hard to stop thinking about it afterward."—*Polityka*

DID THIS HAND KILL?

CEZARY ŁAZAREWICZ

Translated by Sean Gasper Bye

OPEN LETTER
LITERARY TRANSLATIONS FROM THE UNIVERSITY OF ROCHESTER

Originally published in Polish as *Koronkowa robota. Sprawa Gorgonowej* by Wydawnictwo
Czarne, 2018

Library of Congress Cataloging-in-Publication data: Available.
ISBN Paperback: 978-1-948830-79-9
ISBN eBook: 978-1-948830-92-8

*This project is supported in part by an award from the New York State Council on the Arts with
the support of the governor of New York and the New York State Legislature*

Printed on acid-free paper in the United States of America

Cover design by Daniel Benneworth-Gray

Photographs printed by agreement with Czarne and Agencja Wyborcza.pl

Open Letter is the University of Rochester's nonprofit, literary translation press:
Dewey Hall 1-219, Box 278968, Rochester, NY 14627

www.openletterbooks.org

DID THIS HAND KILL?

TRANSLATOR'S NOTE

Cezary Łazarewicz is one of Poland's most prominent contemporary journalists. He broke new ground with his book *To Leave No Trace* (*Żeby nie było śladów*, 2016), about the brutal 1983 murder by police of Grzegorz Przemyk—a student and the son of a Solidarity activist—and the subsequent coverup. The book became the first reportage title to win Poland's top literary prize, the Nike, in 2017. Łazarewicz is a prolific writer and has developed something of a specialty in such historical "cold cases," including the murder of Chris Hani in South Africa by the far-right Polish immigrant Janusz Waluś, and the mysterious death of the opposition activist Stanisław Pyjas in Kraków in 1977.

One of Poland's most notorious criminological mysteries is the murder of Lusia Zarembianka in the small town of Brzuchowice in 1931. The conviction of her father's mistress, Rita Gorgonowa, on circumstantial evidence amid an all-consuming media whirlwind, and Gorgonowa's subsequent mysterious disappearance during the Second World War, have made the case an enduring cultural phenomenon in Poland. Yet over the decades, the details of the trial have fallen into obscurity, while advances in forensic science have raised the prospect of resolving Gorgonowa's guilt or innocence, even nearly a hundred years after the events.

In *Did This Hand Kill?*, Łazarewicz sets out to present the case anew, looking at it through modern eyes. This, to me, is what made the book so well-suited for an international audience. The world of interwar Poland is distant and somewhat mysterious to today's Polish readers, as it also is to Anglophones. So Łazarewicz embarks on recreating not just the facts of the case, but the whole atmosphere of life in newly independent Poland, a country rebuilding its institutions and identity in the aftermath of more than a century of foreign occupation. He shows us a unique, dynamic, and remarkably modern period, whose courtroom dramas and mass media spectacles seem so reminiscent of our own.

For me as a translator, a major task was capturing the plainness and immediacy of Łazarewicz's writing as well as the style and diction of pre-war speech and tabloid journalism. I looked to crime journalism of the era in English (particularly coverage of the Lindburgh kidnapping trial) for inspiration. One challenge was finding suitable legal and courtroom terminology in English, since the Polish system differs significantly from the American. This, however, provided ample opportunity for the sort of nerdy, hair-splitting research that, to me, makes translating non-fiction so much fun.

One area that required a translator's judgment call was to do with place names. Much of this story takes place in Galicia, a historically multiethnic and multilingual region, where history, identity, and territory are often contested, and places and people use different names, or versions of their names, in different languages. Over the course of Łazarewicz's book, we see the Zarembas' home city under Austrian, Polish, and finally Ukrainian rule. But its name would have remained consistent in a given language: in Polish, it has always been (and still is) Lwów; in Ukrainian it has always been (and still is) Lviv. So what should I call it in English?

My thinking here has inevitably been shaped by the context of the full-scale Russian invasion of Ukraine in 2022. This is a war in no small part about Ukrainian identity—about whether Ukraine exists as a country, whether Ukrainian exists as a language, whether Ukrainians exist as a people. In this context, using Ukrainian forms of place names, such as Kyiv rather than the Russian-derived Kiev, becomes an important act of solidarity.

Yet this book's historical context, I felt, called for a different approach. My ultimate decision was to use Polish place names in the historical sections and Ukrainian names in the modern ones, in an effort to build authentic atmospheres for these two time periods. Lviv was a majority-Polish city until the Second World War, when it came under Soviet rule and its ethnically Polish population was expelled. When Łazarewicz visits the city today, it is one that has undergone a profound shift in identity, and so I use Ukrainian toponyms to reflect that. My thanks to the wonderful translator Nina Murray, herself a native of Lviv, for helping me to solidify this approach.

I would also like to thank Cezary Łazarewicz for patiently answering my translation questions, Walker Rutter-Bowman for his insightful editing, and Antonia Lloyd-Jones (as ever) for her support and guidance. Last but not least, my great thanks to Chad Post and Kaija Straumanis, for seeing a place for this book—and for contemporary Polish reportage—in English.

Sean Gasper Bye
Philadelphia and Warsaw
2023

VILLA MAP

•••••• : Gorgonowa's alleged path on the night of the murder

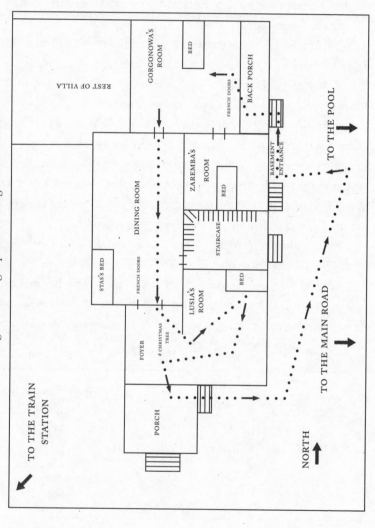

TO THE TRAIN STATION

REST OF VILLA

GORGONOWA'S ROOM

BED

BACK PORCH

FRENCH DOORS

DINING ROOM

STAS'S BED

FRENCH DOORS

ZAREMBA'S ROOM

BED

STAIRCASE

LUSIA'S ROOM

BED

FOYER

CHRISTMAS TREE

PORCH

BASEMENT ENTRANCE

TO THE POOL

TO THE MAIN ROAD

NORTH

To Mom

PROLOGUE

Ever since I was little, I've heard about Gorgonowa. The woman never had a first name. Only a last one. That's also how my grandmother referred to her. Grandma was in Chełm in Lublin Province before the war and lived and breathed the infamous trial. To her, Gorgonowa had always been a victim, a wronged woman caught up in a horrendous crime. The guilty one was the gardener who—Grandma claimed—had confessed·on his deathbed to murdering Lusia.

Forty years later, I read in the paper that Gorgonowa's daughter was fighting to clear her mother's name; it instantly brought back my grandma's stories. I went to Trzebiatów, near the Baltic coast, to do a long interview with the daughter for a news site.

By then, Ewa Ilić was eighty-three and at the center of a media whirlwind. She was fighting to overturn her mother's pre-war conviction and clear her name. She told the story of the night of December 30–31, 1931, and the murder of Lusia Zarembianka, as though it were yesterday and she'd seen it all with her own eyes. She believed her mother was innocent, but couldn't prove it. She kept throwing out new leads and theories that might be worth checking. The media once again debated whether it was Gorgonowa who'd killed Lusia, or someone else.

I decided to find out for myself.

PART I

1931–1933

LUSIA MURDERED

Brzuchowice, night of Wednesday, December 30 to Thursday, December 31, 1931

It comes hurtling out of the darkness and flies straight at him. It's small and very colorful. The engineer's clouded mind tells him it's a hummingbird. He saw one like it in some book. Maybe in Trzaska, Evert, and Michalski's encyclopedia? It has turquoise feathers, an orange beak, and a little black tail.

But how has it ended up in Galicia, at the foot of the Carpathian Mountains, in the middle of a snowy, freezing winter? Even he, an architectural engineer, knows hummingbirds live in the rainforests of South America. He wonders this as he gazes at his large, wrinkled palm, from which the bird picks up a seed, then flies up to his mouth, trying to push it in under his salt-and-pepper mustache.

And then its turquoise feathers turn gray, its beak curls, its claws sharpen, its head and body swell. It's no longer a hummingbird but a vulture. Its ashen wings are so huge they obscure the sky. It drives its sharp talons into the engineer's chest and tries to slash through his neck with its hooked beak. Before the blood comes gushing out, the scream of a fourteen-year-old boy rips through the dream. It's Staś— the engineer's son. Howls and wails are coming from his room. He can't make out the words yet, but their meaning is clear: Staś is calling for help.

17

"I thought he'd gotten sick, fallen, injured himself, that I had to save him," the engineer wrote later.

He leaps out of bed and runs, but the murk in the doorway of the next room stops him short. This room belongs to Rita, his life partner, and mother of their three-and-a-half-year-old daughter, Romusia, who tonight is sleeping in a crib beside the engineer.

The dark is tempered slightly by the pale light reflecting off the December snow from a bulb at the nearby military police outpost. In Rita's room the engineer can make out an indistinct outline of gray against the large porch window. This is an important detail, which he will later be questioned about by investigators, lawyers, judges, journalists. He will never be able to describe it exactly. One time, he says it was a black mass by the porch door; another, a hunched figure squeezed between the bed and the dressing table.

"I didn't think it could be her," he wrote later. "The blackness of the night, emphasized by the blackness of that indistinct shape right through my door, made me realize I'd need to examine the boy in the light."

He retreats to the nightstand by his bed and, hands trembling, so clumsily lights a candle in a holder that he knocks over a glass of water. (The broken glass will be yet another important detail in a pyramid of circumstantial evidence constructed later.)

He runs barefoot with the little flame through Rita's room to the dining room with its large table and fireplace.

Staś's divan bed is on the right, tucked into the alcove under the window. The boy is walking barefoot around the room and wailing:

"Lu-sia's been mur-dered. Mur-derrrred. Muuuuur-derrrrrred."

Elżbieta, known as Lusia, is Staś's seventeen-year-old sister. She sleeps in a pink room behind French doors. Her clothes are stuffed into an enormous, dark-wood wardrobe standing to the right of the entrance. Despite the cold, a vent in the Venetian window is open. Beneath the window is a table with ski gloves lying on it. The skis are leaning against the wall.

In the right corner, a desk heaped with school texts and note-books. It's winter vacation, so the girl hasn't opened them.

Small paintings hang on the wall: landscapes and flowers.

On the left stands the bed. Heavy, steel, pushed right up against the wall. Underneath, a vanity box and a large, leather suitcase.

Before going to sleep Lusia laid her rings, the strap with her key on it, and an unfinished book on her nightstand, where the engineer now places the candlestick. Only then does he notice his daughter's bloodied face. She lies unmoving on her back, with a pillow thrown onto her legs. Her right leg is extended, her left slightly drawn up. Her right arm and clenched fist are cast behind her head, her left arm is at her side. In the faint light he can't yet see that the whole mattress is soaked with blood, dripping crimson onto the wood floor, form-ing a puddle under the bed. Later, a medical expert called in from Lwów—Dr. Dawidowicz—will describe the scene more precisely.

For now, it's the middle of the night. The forty-eight-year-old architectural engineer Henryk Zaremba stands by his daughter's bed, takes her hand, touches her bloodied forehead, and shouts to Staś, who is standing behind him:

"A doctor! Water!"

Their maid, Marcelina Tobiaszówna, brings water.

Zaremba wets some rags and uses them to wipe his daughter's bloodied face. Staś bends her arms back, tries chest compressions.

Rita, whom Zaremba observes out of the corner of his eye, doesn't come near the bed. She stands in the alcove in the foyer. She's wear-ing green slippers and a heavy, brown fur coat with a collar. She watches from afar, as if afraid to come into Lusia's room.

"It didn't even occur to me at the time to take a close look at her face," he later wrote. The only thing that nags at him is that fur coat, since he and Staś are still barefoot in long nightshirts, and there she is already wrapped up and in slippers.

"At times like this is there any room for modesty?" he wonders. "Must you put on a fur coat when someone shouts 'murder?'"

When he comes across Rita a moment later in the dining room, she avoids his gaze but is warm-hearted. She throws her arms around his neck and strokes his head, trying to still his quivering body.

"Henryk darling," she whispers in his ear. "I'm worried about you. Pull yourself together. What's done can't be undone."

Henryk darling doesn't reply.

"How easy to say 'what's done,'" he wrote. "Easy for her, not for a father. I couldn't go back to bed, could I?"

He tells her to fetch the doctor.

Forty-five-year-old Dr. Ludwik Csala is a specialist in internal and pediatric medicine. He is the Zarembas' neighbor. He lives in a red-brick house across Marszałkowska Street. Rita knows him a little because two years ago she went to see him when Romusia was sick. She turns on her heel and goes out. She doesn't take the shortest route past Lusia's room, but instead crosses through the dining room, her room, and the small porch. By walking the length of the building to reach the gate, she adds a considerable distance. Why? This is one of the questions that she will soon need to answer convincingly.

The gate is locked. She goes back. The second exit is on the opposite end of the garden, next to the cottage where the gardener Józef Kamiński and his wife, Rozalia, live. Rita knocks on the window to wake him up.

"Groundskeeper," she shouts, "get up, something terrible's happened!" She asks him to open the back gate for her, but the sleepy gardener discovers that the key that always hangs near it has disappeared.

Rita returns to the villa, takes the spare key from the nail in the kitchen, and runs with it back to the main gate.

Dr. Csala's house looks like it's under construction. The windows on the south wing are boarded up. A painted, metal sign on the gate says to enter from the direction of the nearby cross.

It's nearly one in the morning. Dr. Csala isn't asleep, though he is already in bed; he hears a commotion from outside. The doctor's cart driver comes into the bedroom and informs him that the noise is the neighbor asking for help.

"Why she didn't run straight to me, I don't know," he wonders later. Dr. Csala dresses, then he and his driver head for the villa. The gardener is standing in front of the gate. He's holding a barking dog by the collar so it doesn't jump at them.

The doctor sees Zaremba by the girl's bed, murmuring:

"Save her, doctor."

Dr. Csala remembers the blood caked on the girl's face.

He goes up to the bed, takes her by the hand, tries to find a pulse. He places an ear to her chest, then looks straight into the engineer's pained face.

He says: "I'm afraid there's no saving a corpse."

Zaremba bursts into tears. The doctor takes him by the hand and leads him out. The engineer tries to wrap his mind around everything that's happened in his house in the last hour. He can't understand who shot his daughter and why. He's been sure she was killed by a bullet ever since he noticed the open window in her room.

How did the murderer get into the house? Through the window? The door? The porch? The kitchen? Nothing seemed possible.

As Rita was running to fetch Dr. Csala, Zaremba ordered the gardener to go to the police station in Brzuchowice, two kilometers away, to inform them about Lusia's murder. Kamiński was frightened, he refused. He only agreed to go to the nearby military police station, just beyond the gates of the villa, the place where a light had been on all night. Staś went with him.

The gardener's pounding on the door awakens the thirty-five-year-old sergeant. "Mr. Trela, please get up, there's been a murder. The boss is asking."

Kamiński leads Trela to the house, telling him about the young woman. The snow isn't letting up.

Zaremba greets the sergeant on the porch.

Zaremba will remember him as "an average soldier, crude, and truly unsuited for handling a case of this nature."

They go into the girl's room. The light of the gas lamp is weak, so Trela pulls out his duty flashlight. He shines it around the room, looking for signs of a break-in and anywhere someone might have entered the house. He asks about the open window, though it's only thirty-eight centimeters wide—too small for an adult person to squeeze through. In any case, there are no signs on the windowsill or on the dusty floor of anyone trying to force it open. It's similar outside. The window is fairly high up, so if someone tried to get in, they would have to step in the snow. But it's pristine. Still, Zaremba insists that burglars killed his daughter. He and the sergeant search for traces of them outside by the porch.

"Here!" he shouts to Trela and tells him to follow the footprints.

The sergeant shines the way with his flashlight. The impressions in the snow are small and round, as if made by women's slippers with no heels. (That's how the military policeman describes them in his testimony.) They aren't especially distinct because the snow has filled them in. There are no photos of them because they melted before the police arrived in the morning.

The footprints lead along the eastern wall of the building to the pool. That's what the household calls the cement basin the children splash around in during the summer. Now it looks like a skating rink. The gardener has hacked a hole in the ice and uses it to draw water for the property.

Across from the pool is a cellar. The footprints lead there, too.

"Someone hid in there!" shouts Zaremba to Trela.

The sergeant pulls his loaded revolver from its holster and slowly makes his way down the stairs. The lock is damaged; to get inside they have to shove the door open. To the left and right is space for coal, and straight ahead, the dormant stove for the central heating. But there's no trace of a burglar.

The footprints continue alongside the house to the small porch next to Rita's room.

"It's simple, you see," the engineer explains to the slow-witted military policeman. "As he ran along the wall of the house, past the cellar and the pool, he crossed the small porch and jumped over the wall."

Zaremba's villa is surrounded by a high, two-meter wall, and in some places, a chain-link fence. Near the small porch is where the wall is shortest. It's logical that the burglar picked this particular spot to get into the garden. Here, in the deep, fluffy snow, there should be more footprints.

The sergeant searches for them with groundskeeper Kamiński and Staś. They probe the area around the fence but don't see anything.

It looks as though the perpetrator reached the steps of the small porch and then vanished, because everything ends at that spot.

"We couldn't find anything," they report back to the father.

"I was dejected," Zaremba wrote later. "No one would find my child's killer."

An hour later, Sergeant Trela makes a phone call to the office of ammunition depots a kilometer away. He asks the duty officer of the State Police in Lwów for help. He says seventeen-year-old Elżbieta, daughter of the architect Zaremba, has been murdered in Brzuchowice. The duty officer immediately alerts the policemen at the station in nearby Rzęsna Polska, as well as Józef Frankiewicz, chief of the Lwów County Police. Within twenty minutes, Senior Commissioner Frankiewicz is in his car, along with two detectives—Aspirant Bolesław Respond and Sergeant Walenty Lorch—on their way to Brzuchowice. The weather is abysmal. Snow covers the road, so the ten-kilometer drive, usually less than twenty minutes, takes them almost an hour and a half. At one point they lose their way; they zig-zag, unable to find the villa. Finally, they leave the car in the forest and continue on foot.

They don't reach the villa in Brzuchowice until 4 A.M. Two officers from Rzęsna Polska are already there—Senior Constable Gustaw Szwajcer and Sergeant Józef Nuckowski—as well as two night guards who have been placed outside Lusia's room.

The head of the household sits at the large table in the dining room. He's wearing a short, black fur coat. At the sight of the policemen from Lwów, he lifts his face from his hands.

"Some bandits have murdered my daughter," he says, suddenly energetic.

The investigators remind Zaremba of Laurel and Hardy. The fat, older one is Frankiewicz; the skinny, younger one is Respond. They're both tactful, gentle. They even sit down at the table to offer Zaremba support.

They go everywhere together. They peek into every nook, every cranny. They spend a long while examining the body and conferring. Sometimes they pester Zaremba about something—for instance, whether he's wealthy, or whether he keeps money at home. ("I keep it in a bank in Lwów," he replies, unsure what his daughter's death might have to do with his bank deposits). Then the older one says something Zaremba can't understand: that he should make the investigation easier for them and behave "like a man."

"My God!" worries the engineer. "How can I make it easier? I don't know anything."

At 7:42, it starts growing light in Brzuchowice. Frankiewicz and Respond discover spots of blood on the walls of Lusia's room. Again they go to the engineer. They're no longer sympathetic and kind. They are brusque, cold, unfriendly.

"Mr. Zaremba, this was no bandit attack," Frankiewicz explains to him. "You ought to know best who had an interest in murdering your child. You had better start talking."

Zaremba's eyes grow wide:

"No one had an interest in murdering Lusia," he tells the detective.

That line doesn't please the inspectors. They have him taken into his room and they post a uniformed officer to guard the door. He's not to let Zaremba out of his sight.

"Oh God," thinks Zaremba, "what do they want from me?"

No one tells him anything. No one asks him anything. They just tell him to stay in his room and wait for the prosecutors.

Respond picks them up in Lwów and they arrive after nine o'clock. There are two of them—Junior Prosecutor Emil Krynicki and Investigating Judge Zdzisław Kulczycki.

Zaremba can't understand any of this. Instead of searching for the attacker, one prosecutor asks a policeman if the engineer is well isolated.

"I was sitting alone—holding my aching, uncomprehending head in my hands. When would they finish with these protocols of theirs? And what was all this leading to?"

He hears the footsteps of dozens of people crisscrossing the villa. Chatter, shouts, orders. Through the window, he sees a fire truck driving into the back yard. The firemen park by the pool, pull out their hoses and drain it. What are they looking for there?

The next moment the crowd of people who until then had been standing by the pool burst into his room. They tell him to take off his nightshirt. He stands naked before them and they look him over him like a sculpture in a museum. They carefully inspect his hands, feet, buttocks.

They ask where the ruby-red spots on his nightshirt came from.

"Their stubborn, incomprehensible hostility did not subside," recalls Zaremba. "It seemed even more intense."

Zaremba asks the prosecutor:

"Please let me give my child something to eat!"

"She can wait!" replies Krynicki.

At 3:34 P.M., the sun is setting over Brzuchowice. A caravan of cars is parked in the yard. At five o'clock the investigators summon Zaremba to the pink room. They tell him he may say goodbye to his daughter. (Beside the bed stands an open coffin, shortly into which they will transfer the body.)

Lusia lies corpse-pale on the bloody sheets, while prosecutors, police officers, and court recorders stand around the bed. Junior Prosecutor Krynicki has thought up this trap. He believes the murderer won't be able to stand such pressure and will snap once he approaches his victim. He'll betray himself with a gesture or a word.

So they lead Zaremba straight to the head of the bed. Everyone looks at him intently. Tears are streaming down the engineer's face as he stands beside his daughter's corpse. Then he falls to his knees, leans over the dead girl, pushes back her hair, and kisses her cold forehead.

"Goodbye, Lusia, my friend," he sobs, whimpers, moans, falling into ever greater hysteria.

He clings to the girl so tightly that the policemen have to drag him away.

Rita watches this farewell as if from behind glass. Her cold face shows no emotion. She doesn't really know how she should act. She's afraid to go up to the body, so she stands petrified, wordless.

"Go ahead, ma'am," says Krynicki, encouraging her to come closer. "You won't see her again."

Rita bends over the body and quickly kisses her forehead.

"Lusia, my poor girl," she says. "God knows what's happened to you."

"They were betting both consciences would waver. Neither of ours did, not mine, not Gorgonowa's," wrote Zaremba.

As the engineer was being led out of Lusia's room, he heard Gorgonowa raise her voice:

"Show me your proof that I'm guilty!" she shouted at the police captain.

"I understood why she might also be angry," wrote Zaremba, "since they had prejudged her too, after all."

That evening, the investigators sit down at the large table in the dining room. Emil Krynicki paces between Laurel and Hardy, confidentially whispering something in their ears and time and again glancing suspiciously at the engineer hunched in a corner of the room.

"What does this man really want from me?" wonders Zaremba. "Why won't he release me and leave me to suffer my awful pain alone? Could he suspect that I'm complicit in my own daughter's death, in conspiracy with some sort of bandits over her life?"

"Mr. Zaremba!" says Krynicki sarcastically, "you've got such strong hearing, but you didn't hear the windowpane smash. It's hard to believe!"

"I looked at him in amazement, as at a man with his mind set on tormenting me for no discernible reason. [. . .] Would I have deliberately obstructed the search for the killers of my own dear child?"

Krynicki says something else, something completely absurd and incomprehensible. Something that will weigh on the engineer's mind for days, weeks, and years to come.

"If you didn't have the money, you should have given her this villa."

"What is this fool talking about?" I thought. "Why is he sticking his nose into that? Why is he discussing my material conditions, my domestic relationships, what does any of that have to do with this case?"

By midnight the house is teeming with people. A crowd drawn to Brzuchowice by gossip spends the entire day waiting at the fence, patiently in the cold, for news from inside. They watch the comings and goings, their eyes following the cars as they drive off one by one. Then they can finally go in and look around. They poke their heads into the rooms. A cacophony of voices: in Polish, Russian, Ukrainian, Yiddish. They've come to see the corpse but are disappointed, for Lusia's body has long since gone to the morgue in Lwów. The investigators have even removed the blood-soaked mattress and bed. The only objects of interest are the dark-brown spots on the wall in Lusia's room, the engineer, and his woman. They stare at her like she's

Marlene Dietrich at a première at Lwów's Apollo Cinema, and they comment out loud on what's happened.

"[To them] I was a gorilla to stare at in a cage, a wax figure, I was nothing," recalls Zaremba. "I was overcome with pity and scorn for this intelligent and semi-intelligent rabble."

Most of them are reporters from the Lwów newspapers. Zaremba recognizes them by the notebooks in their hands. They scamper after Laurel and Hardy, who are acting like guides on a school field trip to a museum, stopping at the more important exhibits: Staś's bed, the smashed window in Rita's room, the partially open vent in Lusia's room. The detectives tell the bloody story as if everything were already clear, as if they know what happened. Zaremba can't hear what they're saying, but he can guess it must be important because the visitors are jotting everything down in their notebooks. Thanks to their detailed notes, by tomorrow Lwów's citizens will learn of the den of iniquity in Brzuchowice, the tainted master-builder and the wicked governess in love with him. The first episode of a soap opera that will last until modern times.

"It was just the two of us left," recalls Zaremba, "helpless, not speaking to one another, separated by the guards, awaiting our fate."

He described the scene:

> Once the awaited command arrived from Lwów, the order went out: "Let's go!" They started sealing up the villa. I was departing with my heart in my throat. I felt a deafening roar in my ears—my temples were throbbing.
>
> My horses, ordered from Lwów, were waiting. Four of us got into the coach. Gorgonowa and a policeman were placed on the main seat—on a small bench across from them, the other policeman and I. We rode in silence—it was a wintery night. In the dark I couldn't make out the face of my companion

in misery. In any event, I wasn't interested in her. I was thinking of Lusia and of something incomprehensible, strange, monstrous, that . . . somewhere, the autopsy of her body was taking place, that I, her father, would not even be at her funeral, that because my daughter had been murdered, a policeman was gripping me, her father, so firmly by the arm. [. . .]

The four of us rode like that through the city. The snow lay white on the streets. The stars glistened. Crowds were drifting around. There was a New Year's Eve atmosphere in the air, but we were heading to the municipal police headquarters.

Finally, after that ride—as long as eternity to me— we stopped somewhere at a gate. We walked across a courtyard, plodding through snow. And again, in the darkness, we didn't speak a single word.

I was separated from her by my selfish pain—I was the father of a murdered daughter—I had no words. But why did she not say a single word to me?

The policeman walked alongside me—and she followed with the other. Before us was the black stationhouse.

A two-story building at the corner of Łącki and Sapieha Streets houses the local State Police headquarters, the District Investigative Office and State Police Station No. 6. An annex holds a jail. But before the coach's passengers are sent there, they have to stop by the interrogation room.

They lead Henryk to a brightly lit office and sit Rita down on a bench outside, facing the door.

Material evidence is laid out on a table: bloodied fragments of glass, an ice-axe, a moist handkerchief found in the cellar.

Zaremba is interrogated by the same men he met at the villa: fat Frankiewicz and skinny Respond.

They ask Zaremba if he suspects anyone. Could his daughter have let the attacker in herself?

Could someone manage to squeeze through the narrow window vent? Why didn't the dog bark?

"Mr. Zaremba, screw your head on and think as hard as you can," says Respond, his eyes drilling into him.

"For God's sake," swears the prisoner, "What would I be hiding?"

"Come on now, admit it," presses Respond.

"Admit what?" says Zaremba, amazed.

"That you're protecting Gorgonowa."

("It was as if a lightning bolt had struck within me. I was seized with terror. My shoulders hunched . . . as if a mountain were pressing down on me . . . It couldn't be her!" Zaremba would later write.)

The first interrogation of Henryk Zaremba ends at five in the morning.

"We're very sorry," says Respond as they say goodbye, "but we have to take you to the jail."

Zaremba: "I said nothing. My thoughts were chaos, a whirl of bloody shreds. I gazed at them with unseeing eyes. The world had collapsed on top of me."

Rita's interrogation takes even longer. During this time, Zaremba waits in the hallway outside the office. Finally the door opens, revealing Gorgonowa.

"You told them you think I did it!" she says, angrily accusing the engineer.

Zaremba doesn't reply.

They no longer speak to one another as a policeman leads them across the courtyard through the slushy snow to the jail.

"I was reeling from a powerful blow," recalls the engineer. "I was thinking of Lusia, not myself, not her."

The jail guard slides open the bars of the women's section and politely invites Gorgonowa in:

"You first, ma'am."

"Defend me." That is her final request, made to Zaremba as they part. Before he can say anything, the steel bars slam shut behind her.

They lead him further down a long corridor, at the end of which is a heavy door with a Judas hole. Before the guard closes the door behind Henryk Zaremba, he raises a hand to his throat and runs a finger across his Adam's apple.

Out the barred window, Lwów glitters in the light of all its streetlamps—897 electric and 3,917 gas.

THE SUSPECTS

Margarita Emilia Gorgonowa, née Ilić, age thirty.

Build—slim.

Height—165 centimeters.

Hair—dark (brunette).

Face—oval.

Eyes—blue.

Eyebrows—curved.

Nose—medium.

Teeth—complete set.

After being interrogated further, she is taken to the prison on Lwów's Kazimierzowska Street, which has stood since the eighteenth century on the site of a former Brigittine convent, and so is known as Brygidki.

It mainly holds political prisoners, shop-window-smashing members of the Communist Party of Western Ukraine, and bomb-planting rebels from the Ukrainian Nationalist Organization.

Gorgonowa is put in a six-person cell with Polish communists. Political prisoners have privileges in the jails of interwar Poland, they can lie on their cots during the day, they have their own small library and access to newspapers. With the arrival of this new detainee, a suspect of a simple criminal act, those privileges are suspended.

Newspapers are particularly restricted, to prevent her from learning too much about the case against her. The communists protest the restrictions and Rita is transferred to another cell.

Henryk Mikołaj Zaremba, age forty-eight.
    Build—stocky.
    Height—174 centimeters.
    Hair—none.
    Forehead—high.
    Face—oval.
    Eyes—hazel.
    Eyebrows—straight.
    Ears—large.
    Teeth—complete set.
He is also held in Brygidki, but in cell 118, which he shares with two Ukrainians and one Jew. They are suspected of seditious activity—and he of being an accessory to his daughter's murder.

"They were good people," he wrote of his fellow prisoners. "They were interested in me as a person, my suffering, they could tell right away I was only an unlucky father. They possessed a perceptiveness of heart, they knew a great deal about miscarriages of justice and victims of the 'law.' Without the sympathy of these men I would surely have lost my mind."

Henryk is subject to a strict regime. Reveille at 6 A.M., handing over your pants at 8 P.M., lights out and quiet time at 9 P.M. Every time he leaves for interrogation by the investigating judge, a guard pats him down under the armpits, in front, in back. He tells him to turn out his pockets.

"As if I had stolen something and were hiding it," he notes.

Zaremba also has privileges. They allow visitors to bring him meals from the city and he may use a fork and knife. Other prisoners eat with spoons. Yet before going to bed he must return his utensils to the guard, along with his pants.

He also has the right to a one-hour walk outside the building, which he never takes. He explains his reluctance:

"I prefer the filth of a sticky floor, the mustiness of a cell, squashing bedbugs on the wall, to walking in a circle in a little scrap of yard under the eyes of prisoners curious to get a peek at Zaremba."

When on the Saturday just after his arrest the prison office asks him for instructions for his daughter's funeral, Zaremba is helpless. He weeps. He protests that he has no money. He asks them to pawn one of his paintings so he can cover the cost of the ceremony.

Journalists write that he is completely broken.

THE ORIGIN OF A VILLAINESS

Lwów, Thursday, December 31, 1931

On New Year's Eve on elegant Akademicka Street, militants from the Communist Party of Western Ukraine scattered pamphlets and then smashed windows at the Roma café and the Wedel chocolate shop; in a courtyard entryway at 68 Stryjeńska Street, eighteen-year-old Franciszka Można poisoned herself with iodine; and in an apartment at 38 Gispowa Street, Mieczysław Kędzierski tried to take his life by downing a bottle of methylated spirit.

On Zamarstynowska Street, Maria Watenberg and her six-year-old son were run over by a taxi, and the safecracker Mojżesz Gross, who lived on the same street but at number 14, was arrested by detectives on suspicion of breaking into the vault of the Credit Bank in nearby Złoczów.

But nothing gets people so worked up as the news emerging from the villa of a well-known local architect, Engineer Henryk Zaremba. Even on New Year's Eve, Lwów hears rumors of his daughter Elżbieta Zarembianka's murder, but not until the next day can they read about it in the press.

Gazeta Lwowska is the first to report on Lusia's death: "The suspicion arises that this crime was committed by a nursery maid in service to Engineer Zaremba for several years, with whom he has maintained a romantic relationship for an extended period. This nursery maid likely wished to end Elżbieta's life because she was an obstacle to Engineer Zaremba obtaining a divorce from his spouse."

This is precisely the moment when thirty-year-old Margarita Emilia Gorgonowa becomes the most villainous of villains. With each passing day, her image will grow more sinister, her likeness multiplied in hundreds of thousands of copies and sold all over Poland.

In the fourteen years since Polish independence, Lwów has had great trials that riveted the entire country. One such trial was in 1921, when the Ukrainian nationalist Stepan Fedak fired a gun at Chief of State Józef Piłsudski in front of Lwów City Hall; another was three years later, when Stanisław Steiger was accused of the attempted assassination of President Stanisław Wojciechowski.

In the late twenties, Lwów was gripped by the shooting on Królewska Street of the city's school superintendent Stanisław Sobiński (his killers' trial would drag on until 1929), and in fall of 1931, by the murder of the trolly conductor Rudolf Koszyczek, whose wife stabbed him to death in their shared apartment.

Yet nothing can equal the fever that raged after the killing of Lusia Zarembianka. Lwów is hungry for information about the main figures in the tragedy: Rita, the engineer, and his unfortunate daughter. Every detail of their lives is now probed, weighed, and analyzed in the most minute detail. No secret is safe from gossip dragging it out into the open.

New witnesses are continually turning up at newspaper offices, telling unbelievable stories about the couple's life; the newspapers launch their own investigations, hunting for new circumstances, witnesses, suspects. When they go too far, exposing nuances of the investigation, the courts step in and confiscate entire print runs. (Shortly after Gorgonowa and Zaremba's arrest, a Lwów court requisitioned the entire print runs of two separate press titles in a single day. In the judges' view the publications were inappropriately interfering in the legal proceedings.)

Lwów's *Słowo Polskie* writes that the maid Olga Jezierska's testimony should absolutely contribute to the rich material evidence against Gorgonowa. The newspaper tracked down Jezierska, and she recounted how Gorgonowa threatened Lusia Zarembianka's life and intended to kill a small, domesticated roe deer that the girl loved. First she tried to enlist Jezierska, but when the maid refused, Gorgonowa declared she'd cut off the animal's head herself. "You just have to help me hold it down while I slaughter it," she'd said.

Jezierska tells the journalists that her mistress "was vengeful, ruthless, and heartless."

Gazeta Lwowska tracked down another servant, Marcelina Tobiaszówna. She told the journalists that on the unhappy night, as everyone was running to Lusia's pink room, she spotted the Lady. She saw her sit down for a moment at the dining room table, hiding her face in her hands and repeating: "Oh God, oh God, what I have I done?"

Even the famously conscientious *Ilustrowany Kurier Codzienny*, the greatest pre-war newspaper, finds it hard to hold back. They write that jailed Rita is a rarely encountered type of criminal, one with pathological personality traits.

The paper also prints revelations from a certain Lwów newsstand owner and war invalid. He claims that during the last war, when he was serving in the Austro-Hungarian army in Yugoslavia, he came across Gorgonowa in Dalmatia. She was an escort in an Austrian military brothel.

Is this credible, since a few days earlier the same newspaper questioned whether Gorgonowa had ever lived in Dalmatia at all, or if she even knew Serbian?

The evening papers write that she's wicked and vain, and that before she emerges from her cell for interrogation, she always takes her time doing herself up, putting on lipstick, powdering her face, and gazing at herself in the mirror. The "revolver press," as people call it in Lwów, is responding to demand from readers who want to hear about the Zaremba household's moral depravity, to learn details—who did what to whom, with what, and why—to get to know the main characters, to look them in the eyes (the papers try to find photos of Engineer Zaremba, but they can't get a hold of one anywhere), and to judge who is evil and who is good.

Gorgonowa is evil because she entrapped an old man, took advantage of him, maybe at the expense of his children, and finally killed his daughter, who was competing with her.

Zaremba is evil because he let a young lass beguile him. Instead of leading the life of a widower and visiting his sick wife in the hospital, he forgot her and fell in love. Maybe he wasn't complicit in his daughter's murder, but he's covering for his mistress.

Lusia (no one calls her Elżbieta anymore) is good; she was a girl who wanted to free her father from the clutches of her wicked "stepmother," and for that she paid the highest price.

The newspapers turn Gorgonowa into the personification of evil. To hear them tell it, she's more devious than Lady Macbeth and wickeder than Cinderella's stepmother.

They use leaks from the investigation, rumors, and scraps of information to construct a portrait of a monster-woman. They write that her actions were driven by cynicism, that she shows no remorse. That her mouth is curled into a nonchalant smile when she meets with the investigating judge, and a mocking grin appears on her face when she speaks of Lusia's death. "To date, no one in Poland has had such an incredible grip on the public's attention," writes a senior commentator for the conservative *Nowiny Codzienne*.

This frenzy, so often violently controversial, has even infected families. The tremendous majority of the masses at large have their curious eyes fixed on the Gorgonowa Case.

How can we explain this phenomenon?

First and foremost, the general curiosity is strengthened because the criminal suspect is a woman, for women rarely commit murder with their own hands, and when they do commit it directly, it is much more refined.

Second, the mystery factor plays a fascinating role. The secret of the villa has grown so convoluted that the question mark, far from vanishing, is growing bigger and bigger. That it's so hard to get at sources of truth makes the Gorgonowa case a sensation of a special caliber.

But there's still something more, and that's a collective sense of justice. This sense—so strong, often vehement—proves the existence in Poland of a sensitive public conscience, capable of reacting collectively—and very strongly at that.

THE FRANKIEWICZ REPORT

Lwów, Friday, January 1, 1932

Shortly after arriving in Lwów, Senior Commissioner Józef Frankiewicz recreates the last moments in the life of seventeen-year-old Elżbieta Zarembianka, based on witness testimony. His report is one of the more important documents in the investigation, relating the particular course of events and what happened just after the girl's death.

Frankiewicz writes that the family of Engineer Zaremba arrives in Brzuchowice from Lwów on Wednesday, December 23. Each of them already knows this is a farewell gathering. This particular group will probably never be together at the villa again, because the forty-eight-year-old engineer has decided to break up with his partner, who is eighteen years his junior. The die was cast about two weeks before, when Zaremba rented out a four-room apartment in a low-rise at 71 Potocki Street—one too small for Rita and their four-year-old daughter to live in too. So, only the children from his first relationship—seventeen-year-old Lusia and her brother Stanisław, three years younger—will move to Potocki Street with him. Now they're just waiting for word from the current tenants, who are to leave the apartment by January 1 at the latest.

As a result Rita and Romusia must abandon the shared seven-room apartment rented at 8 Dembiński Street and move into Zaremba's house in Brzuchowice. Brzuchowice is an upscale suburb attracting the wealthy of Lwów. There, amid sandy, pine-covered hillocks, they have built their luxurious homes. One of these, on a side street, is Henryk Zaremba's summer home, where Gorgonowa will be able to settle down with their child after the breakup. Since Rita has no job, the engineer has also agreed to support her and their little daughter.

The atmosphere of a relationship on its last legs makes the end of December in the villa a minefield. Arguments constantly break out. Rita's resentment focuses on Zaremba's daughter, who is setting her father against the governess. Gorgonowa doesn't hold back her anger against the girl. Whenever Lusia can, she stays out of Gorgonowa's way, since she knows she won't have to deal with her for much longer. In the morning Lusia takes the train to Lwów to pack her things in the old apartment; she returns in the evening, eats dinner, and goes to bed. She does nothing that might provoke an argument.

LUSIA'S LAST DAY

Wednesday, December 30, 1931

Lusia leaves the house when it's still dark outside. She takes the shortest route to the station, past the gardener's house and through the gate at the back of the garden, where the key is always hanging on a nail. Then she walks a few hundred meters on a forest path to Hołosko train station. (Zaremba's villa lies within the village of Łączki, on the borderline of two townships—Brzuchowice and Hołosko.) The station is made up of two crude wood-plank sheds surrounded by a wooden fence—one shed for the ticket desk, the other for the waiting room. At 6:45, Lusia gets on the first train to Lwów. It's only nine kilometers. The trip—with two stops, in Rzęsna Polska and Kleparów—takes fifteen minutes.

The apartment on Dembiński Street is reachable from the main train station by trolley. It's four stops on the number 2. You have to get out at the last stop, on Gródecka Street.

Dembiński is a small side-street coming off of Bem Square near the former Austrian barracks. Lusia will stay there until evening, packing up her family's possessions.

At nine, Zaremba leaves Brzuchowice. He reaches Lwów by motor coach. His architect's studio is in a two-story tenement at 10 Copernicus Street, across from the modern Copernicus movie theater.

Though it's not far from there to Dembiński Street, he doesn't see his daughter during the day. Lusia phones him around noon. She says she'll make her own way back to the house that evening. She asks if someone can meet her on the platform.

Zaremba takes the train back from Lwów at 3:25. He joins up with Staś and Romusia, who are playing in the snow in the garden. He and the children build a snowman, throw snowballs, pull Romusia on a sled. When it gets dark, they go back to the house and listen to the radio in Zaremba's room with the door closed.

What is Rita up to right now? Zaremba doesn't really care.

"We were avoiding one another," he testified.

He only knows that that morning, right after Lusia left, Rita aired out the girl's room, brought in some water, and started washing the windows.

The train from Lwów arrives at 7:45. A little before that, Staś heads out to the station to collect his older sister from the train. As they make their way back through the woods, the snow is already falling heavily.

Lusia is cheerful. On the way she tells Staś about how she organized things in the apartment in Lwów.

They enter the villa through the kitchen door (the main entrance from the porch is usually locked). Their father, stepmother, and Romusia are already sitting at the dining room table. They aren't talking. He's reading the magazine *Naokoło Świata* ("Around the World"), and she's reading *America* by the popular writer Emil Ludwig. She doesn't even look up from her book as the children say hello.

"Why the long face?" Zaremba asks Rita, but he gets no response.

Rita leaves the dining room before dinner is served. As she leaves, she once again scolds Lusia for losing the shade for a gas lamp and forbids the girl from spending the night with Romusia.

The Zarembas eat meat pierogies. At the table, Lusia tells them about the engraved visiting card with her name that will hang on the door of the new apartment. She's awed that she'll be the most important woman in the household, not this stranger her father brought into their family.

They talk in whispers because Romusia is sleeping in her father's lap. Zaremba does most of the talking—about the Lady's difficult personality, the bad moods she falls into for no reason.

After dinner, the father picks up sleeping Romusia and crosses through Rita's room to his bedroom. Staś and Lusia follow him. Every evening they walk their father to bed. By then, the Lady is already under the covers. She's still reading Ludwig by the light of the gas lamp.

It's very hot in the house, so Staś cracks open the window in his father's room and places a candle holder, matches, and a glass of water on his nightstand. Before leaving he tunes the radio so his father can listen to a holiday concert.

He and Lusia give Henryk a goodnight kiss and leave. As they pass through Rita's room, they say goodnight. She doesn't respond.

Staś closes the door of Rita's bedroom. Lusia takes the newspaper her father left behind and Staś walks her to the pink room. The maid brings the girl a gas lamp and Staś plugs her headphones into the radio. Around nine o'clock he says goodnight to his sister and goes back to the dining room. He can hear Lusia pouring water into a basin and washing up. Staś puts on his headphones, turns on the radio and lies down in the divan bed by the window. Before he falls asleep, he takes one more look at Lusia's room. The lamp is still lit. That's a sign his sister isn't sleeping. *She must be reading* is his last thought before dozing off.

At around 9:30 he falls asleep with his headphones on.

Zaremba is also listening to the radio, and falls asleep around the same time.

At around midnight, the boy is jolted awake by the dog whining.

"As if someone had hit him," he later describes it to the investigators.

He sits up in bed and listens carefully. He thinks it must be someone from the household making noise: if it were a stranger, the dog would bark loudly.

He looks out the window. Outside he can only see white snowflakes falling in the garden. He has the feeling someone is standing behind the glass door in the foyer. He thinks it's his older sister, so he calls out quietly, to be sure: "Lusia, Lusia." The girl doesn't respond. Staś slowly gets up from the divan bed and goes to the French doors separating the dining room from the foyer. He stands a half-pace in front of them. In the darkness he can see the outline of a human figure, five, maybe six paces farther along, between the piano and the large Christmas tree hung with ornaments. The boy nervously taps his knuckles on the glass and calls louder and louder:

"Lusia, Lusia, Lusia." Then he realizes it's not Lusia, but someone taller.

The figure standing motionless in the dark wavers, moves carefully to the left, toward the front door, which swings open for a moment as it slips outside into the garden. For a split second it stands against a background of white snow reflecting the yellow light from the nearby military police station, which allows the boy to perceive the outline of hair and a fur collar (as he will testify later).

And not until the figure disappears out the door does Staś cautiously enter the foyer. He goes straight to his sister's room. Dark. He looks at the bed against the wall and thinks Lusia's not in it. A pillow lies where her head usually is.

He approaches and lifts the pillow, revealing her inert head underneath. He tries shaking his sister awake, but his fingers sink into sticky, warm gunk.

"Lu-sia's been mur-dered. Mur-derrrred. Muuuuur-derrrrrred," he shouts over her still motionless body and runs to wake up his father.

The gardener, Józef Kamiński, is the first person Staś tells about the mysterious figure he saw in the foyer.

"They were wrapped in a fur coat," he explains to Kamiński later that night, as they walk to the military police station to alert them of the murder.

Staś doesn't say who the person was or even if it was a man or a woman. Kamiński doesn't press him. He just repeats to Sergeant Trela everything the boy told him. Trela, meanwhile, reports the puzzling nocturnal visit to police officer Józef Nuckowski once he arrives at the Zarembas' villa. Then Nuckowski passes it on—to Senior Commissioner Frankiewicz.

Early in the morning, Staś finds himself at the military police station again, but this time as a key witness. Aspirant Bolesław Respond questions him.

During this first interrogation, Staś tells Respond an important detail: the figure he saw in the night was a woman. And one more thing: she had long, tousled hair.

The aspirant notices the boy is nervous. He doesn't press him or ask follow-up questions. He eases up.

"I felt like he was holding back, as if he was hiding something. I guessed that before he said anything, he wanted to consult with his father," Respond later testified in court.

A few hours later, Respond once again questions Staś. He asks him directly:

"Did you recognize the figure in the foyer?"

Aspirant Respond calligraphs young Zaremba's statement in black ink:

"Between the piano and the Christmas tree I spotted the silhouette of a woman in a fur coat, standing facing me, whom I recognized as Mrs. Gorgonowa," he writes. "I started knocking on the glass, at which Mrs. Gorgonowa quietly and quickly stepped through the door straight onto the porch, turning left at the door."

Staś continued: "In the dining room I shouted: 'Lusia's been murdered.' At my cry, the first person to come into the dining room was Mrs. Gorgonowa, who was dressed as I had seen her previously, namely in a brown fur coat and with bed slippers on her feet."

(In court, Stanisław Zaremba explains that only after returning from the guard station, some two hours after discovering Lusia's corpse, did the thought first occur to him that the figure was Gorgonowa. He then lay down on the sofa and wondered whether to tell his father. But he didn't even have a chance, because his father was under police guard.)

Staś tells the investigators that after Gorgonowa and his father fell out, Zaremba started sending the household maintenance money to Lusia instead. Gorgonowa, who never had a job, was left without funds for living expenses. She even had to ask Lusia to buy personal items. Rita took this very badly.

The boy talks about the constant arguments and death threats that Gorgonowa directed at his sister.

"I know she was afraid of how vengefully Gorgonowa was acting. She was scared of sleeping alone in her bed and I know she felt in danger of retaliation," testified Staś.

Thanks to the fourteen year old's statements, after a few hours of investigation the police have not only a primary suspect but also a motive for the crime: revenge.

On Friday, January 1, 1932, Senior Commissioner Józef Frank-iewicz stitches the statements together into a convincing story.

He writes that Gorgonowa planned Zaremba's daughter's murder in advance and prepared well for it. So on the evening of Thursday, December 30, when the Zaremba siblings come through her bed-room to say "goodnight," she must have already hidden the ice-axe that she will use two hours later to smash in Lusia's skull.

While lying in bed and reading her book, she is only waiting for everyone else to fall asleep. Once she's sure no one will surprise her, she gets out of bed, puts on her slippers, throws on a heavy, brown fur coat, and sets off through the kitchen past sleeping Staś to Lusia's room. (The investigators do not know, however, whether she brought the axe with her or if it was previously hidden in the pink room.)

Frankiewicz hypothesizes that after the killing, Gorgonowa opens the window in the girl's room to give the impression of a break-in. All of this is to draw suspicion away from the household, deflecting the blame toward an undefined burglar and pervert.

(Two days after Lusia's death, experts discover her hymen is not intact, but since they don't find semen in her vagina, they conclude she was not raped.)

After committing the murder, Gorgonowa intends to retreat unnoticed to her bedroom, but things get complicated when she opens the door to the porch, to make it look like the unknown killer went that way to escape, beccause at that moment, in slips Lux, the German shepherd guarding the Zarembas' property. Gorgonowa, trying to chase him away, hits the dog on the head with the axe. The dog's whining awakens Staś.

The boy gets out of bed and goes up to the French doors, thus blocking the murderer's retreat, forcing her to escape by another route.

Staś enters Lusia's room. As he lifts the pillow, Gorgonowa runs along the house toward the other porch, meanwhile tossing the bloody axe away by the entrance to the cellar. (The police discovered a bloody dent over the door handle.) She can't return to her room because the glass door is locked from the inside. She breaks a pane and turns the key, cutting her hand at the same time. She makes it into her room just as Staś is raising the alarm.

Staś hears the crash of the broken windowpane near the fireplace in the dining room, as he's running from Lusia's room to alert his father. A moment later, Rita is the first to arrive in the living room, pretending she has just jumped out of bed. She's dressed in a fur coat and green slippers, while Zaremba, who runs in just behind her, is barefoot, in a nightshirt.

Then, according to Frankiewicz, the following happened:

> After feigning participation in the rescue operation and running to get the doctor, she did not wait for him there, but returned home, where amid the general chaos, she withdrew from the room where everyone was occupied. She went alone to her bedroom, took a candle from the console table next to the bed, and left her bedroom through the door to the porch, and from there went into the cellar. Having lit the candle, she intended to conceal in the cellar the ice-axe the ice-axe and the bloody handkerchief that she had on her person during the murder and used to wipe off her bloodied hands. After rinsing off the blood, she stuffed the handkerchief into the place where it was later found. Meanwhile, she did not find an appropriate place in the cellar to conceal the ice-axe. Therefore she left the cellar (holding the extinguished candle and candlestick) and, with the ice-axe, made for the adjacent frozen pool, where she decided to submerge the axe in the ice-hole.
>
> She had to bend over the ice-hole. As she did so, the candle, placed loosely in the holder, fell unseen into the snow. The perpetrator, not noticing this in the dark, took the same route back to the bathroom and only then noticed the missing candle; not knowing where to search for it, she moved the empty candle holder, unnoticed, to the hutch in the dining room. Amid the constant confusion in the house at this time, once back in her bedroom Gorgonowa had the opportunity to remove the nightgown she had soiled

and to burn it using propane taken from the kitchen, supposedly for disinfecting her injured hand.

It is not impossible that Henryk Zaremba noticed certain suspicious signs in Gorgonowa during the events surrounding the murder, in her appearance and behavior. Yet because of his love for the child he had with her, he was able to keep these observations to himself.

In his report, Senior Commissioner Frankiewicz even explains the puzzle of the excrement found on the floor. "As she left the room, under the influence of thrill and stress, the suspect endured a tremendous mental shock. Staggering along the wall, she reached the entrance alcove, on which she left very distinct bloody handprints. Coming down the step, her nerves could not hold up and unawares, in a standing position, she defecated."

According to the commander of Lwów's police force, this was the course of events in the killing of young Elżbieta Zarembianka.

The trouble is that what looks fairly convincing on paper may end up difficult to prove. The prime suspect is still denying everything and unwilling to admit her guilt.

The newspapers write that she is completely broken. When she learned she faced execution by hanging, she asked to be shot because, as she explained to the investigators, she is terrified of gallows.

THE GREAT SPECTACLE AT ŁYCZAKÓW CEMETERY

Lwów, Monday, January 4, 1932

Lusia is dressed in a snow-white, lace dress brought by her aunt Maria Kudelkowa to the Institute of Forensic Medicine at 52 Piekarska Street. No one will see the dress—the coffin is closed, because the skin was removed from the girl's face during the autopsy.

Lusia's silver-colored, tin coffin is placed in the crypt of the Bernardine Church. This is the largest church in Lwów, bursting with baroque angels, majestic vaults, gold leaf, and a record-setting eighteen altars.

Since early morning the church has been jammed with people. They've come to bid farewell to the girl whose mysterious death they've been reading about in the papers in recent days.

"The psychosis of collective curiosity drove crowds from the city's most distant neighborhoods to the murdered girl's coffin," writes a reporter for *Gazeta Lwowska*.

To get inside, people have to push through a small, wrought-iron door. Newspaper photos taken at the funeral show us this isn't easy. There's an unbelievable crush on Bernardyński Square around the John of Dukla Column near the front of the church. Everyone is trying to slip through that iron bottleneck and into the church. But that will prove impossible because the narrow corridor leading to the crypt where the coffin is located has been packed since morning. In any case, it will soon be closed off for fear of a catastrophe. This does not discourage the onlookers. They don't yet know the coffin has been sealed, and everyone wants to see the marks the ice-axe left on the girl's head. Trolleys overflowing with people clinging to their sides spit their passengers out on Halicki and Bernardyński Squares. From all directions, processions make their way down narrow side streets, moving toward the same place. By 2 p.m., an hour before Mass is meant to start, the crowds are even denser. A sea of heads from Halicki Square to Pańska Street. The neighboring thoroughfares are also jammed: Wałowa, Sobieski, Sienkiewicz, Czarnecki, and Piłsudski Streets, along which the cortège will run, are under siege. Never before has any funeral, any Mass, sparked such attention.

"Suburban women predominate, often with babes in arms," notes a reporter from *Słowo Polskie*, estimating the crowd at ten thousand.

Police cordons attempt to direct the flow of people, but there's no holding back the pressure. Mounted units go into action, keeping the throng from storming the church. Women squeal and shout as they're chased away.

Słowo Polskie:

> When the hour struck three, the mournful tones of bells reverberated from the church tower. The crowd froze in anticipation. After a moment, from the Bernardine Fathers' crypt rose a pall-draped cross, and behind it, the silver-colored tin coffin. Men removed their hats; the whispers of prayer could be heard. Amid the clergy's mournful singing, the coffin was placed on a hearse hung with wreaths from family, friends, and the Olga Filippi School, where the deceased was in her sixth year of secondary education.

Leading the cortège was Father Stanisław Frankel, accompanied by Bernardine nuns. Processing behind the coffin were the Kudelkas [Maria Kudelkowa is the deceased's aunt], Lusia's brother Stanisław, and her further family.

Bernardyński Square shakes its fists at Gorgonowa, wishing her death. Death to her, and Engineer Zaremba too, whom they consider morally culpable for the murder. They keep an eye out for him among the mourners, because rumor has it he's present. They even attack a car with shrouded windows when a rumor spreads that he's inside.

In lieu of the father, whom Judge Kulczycki has detained in jail, attention focuses on the murdered girl's fourteen-year-old brother. "They want to see little Staś, painfully broken," *Słowo Polskie* reports.

Those who can't squeeze up to the hearse in front of the Bernardine Church now race down side streets to Piekarska Street, along which the cortège will come directly. They push through to get the best spot.

It's about two kilometers from the church to the main gates of Łyczaków Cemetery.

Thousands more of Lwów's citizens wait there. These are the ones who have forced their way through the police cordons, wagering they'll be able to slip into the cemetery. Yet the main gate is locked. The police are guarding it. No one will sneak through here.

At 4 P.M. mounted patrols disperse the onlookers in front of the gates, clearing a path for the hearse and mourners to enter. Zarembianka's grave lies to the right of the main avenue. Plot fifty-three. The place is easy to recognize by the trampled graves all around.

The cemetery is silent as Father Frankel commences the final farewell. It is so quiet that the only sounds heard are of sobbing and the thud of lumps of earth striking the lid.

When dusk falls, the police officers open the cemetery gates wide. Those who have waited there for many hours may now see the grave with their own eyes. It is densely covered in wreaths, with an oaken cross rising above them bearing a white plaque: "Here lies Elżbieta Zarembianka, who died a tragic death in her seventeenth summer of life."

"There is no doubt Gorgonowa murdered Elżbieta," Mayor Paweł Csala of Brzuchowice Township insists to reporters. "You could bet your soul on it," he assures them.

There's widespread confidence that the case is clear-cut. The evidence is strong. The witness testimonies incriminate Gorgonowa. According to the papers, there's no doubt she's guilty.

Therefore, so as not to waste time, the Lwów masses demand a summary trial, meaning at express speed. The Criminal Code dictates that in such cases the investigation must conclude within two weeks, the court has twenty-four hours to set a trial date, and the trial itself must begin no later than three weeks after the suspect's arrest. This simplified procedure means the sentence is delivered not only immediately, but also irrevocably. There's no need to wait weeks for appeals.

Journalists somewhat optimistically estimate that with a little luck everything can be wrapped up by the second half of February. And knowing the efficiency of Lwów's courts, one can presumably they'll have the execution over with by the end of March at the latest.

Tajny Detektyw ("The Secret Detective"), the most popular investigative weekly of interwar Poland, writes that only one thing trou-

DID THIS HAND KILL?

bles the minds of Lwów's citizens: "Might Gorgonowa turn out to be innocent? Could circumstances come to light that cause her to walk free from the jailhouse walls?"

No one, of course, gives that a second thought.

On the day of the funeral, Investigating Judge Zdzisław Kulczycki seizes one more opportunity. At dawn, accompanied by police officers, he sets off for the crypt of the Bernardine Fathers' Church on Bernardyński Square. Just before the service, he orders the coffin opened once again and snips off a lock of Lusia's dark hair.

That very day it's sent to the laboratory. If one of Lusia's hairs is found on Rita's clothes, that will be compelling evidence that on that night, Gorgonowa was in the pink room.

Technicians compare Zarembianka and Gorgonowa's hair under the microscope yet are unable to distinguish them. "There was no way of determining from which of these women they originated," they write in their report.

Two days later, on January 2, doctors draw blood from Gorgonowa to test its type. Murdered Elżbieta is type A—the accused, type O.

If they find factor A on Gorgonowa's clothes or on objects she touched, this will be convincing evidence of her guilt.

There is a large amount of bloodied clothing—from Henryk Zaremba's underwear to Romusia's playsuit to Rita's brassiere. The material evidence is sent not to a specialized facility, but to a Lwów pharmacy's medical and chemical lab. It will be tested by a teacher from a local high school. (One of the main lines of defense will be to question the reliability of these analyses.)

The technicians find factor A on the comforter, pillow, and couch in Lusia's room, and on a match that lay on the nightstand. This goes without saying.

Most of the spots on the walls, door frames, and windows cannot be tested, either because there is insufficient material or, the experts conclude, it has undergone denaturation, as has the blood on the walls of Zarembianka's room. These also have some bloody finger-prints on them, but according to the lab at the Main Police Head-quarters in Warsaw, they belong to Staś.

There are no traces of Lusia's blood on the door handles in Rita's room, nor on Rita's nightgown or brassiere. All this blood is type O, meaning it came from Gorgonowa's injured hand.

Yet the chemists do discover flecks of blood on the lining of the brown fur coat. Someone tried to remove the stain with water, but instead of rubbing it out, they pushed it into the wadding. It is large enough to extract for testing—and it turns out to be type A. This is crucial and strong evidence against Gorgonowa: it shows she must have been standing by Lusia's bed as she was dying.

The coat lining also has a second, larger stain, one showing the presence of fecal components. If the sample of feces from the lining matches the one found at the scene of the crime, it would be more compelling evidence against Gorgonowa. Unfortunately, there is too little material to compare for a thorough analysis.

A week after the crime, the investigators return to Brzuchowice. (Maybe because of the lack of strong material evidence.) Yet again they comb the house and garden in search of the truth behind the incident. They discover, among other things, that some dried blood has been left on the cracked window in the gardener's house that Gorgonowa knocked on in the night. Unfortunately, there is too lit-tle to determine its type.

And that is all of the key material evidence.

GUILTLESS

"Do you admit to murdering Elżbieta Zarembianka?" asks the young assistant judge, Zdzisław Kulczycki, at every interrogation. This case has fallen to Kulczycki almost by accident. (Lawyers of the bar will long marvel at the reckless decision to entrust the case to him of all people, an assistant judge with barely a few months of investigative experience, rather than to someone with many years under his belt.)

Each time Rita replies the same way:

"No. I didn't do it!" Then she asks her interrogator: "Where do these suspicions come from? Who dares suspect me?"

Later, their dialogue goes more or less like this:

"So, who, in your opinion, committed this crime?"

"I don't know. What business of that is mine? That's what the police are for!"

"And what do you say to the evidence we've gathered against you?"

"Nothing. I don't believe it proves me guilty. Maybe it's evidence against someone else."

"Maybe you can tell us whom you suspect of the murder?"

"No. You gentlemen can worry about that yourselves."

"How did the ice-axe get in the pool?"

"What does that have to do with me? The groundskeeper was the one who used it."

"How did the window break?"

"I smashed it with my elbow. It was after the murder was discovered, when my husband shouted: 'Water, water!' I rushed into the yard for water. I wanted to come back through the porch and broke the windowpane to turn the key from the inside."

"Since you broke the window with your elbow, how do you have cuts on your wrist?"

"I cut it while I was clearing out the shards that were left in the window frame."

"Why were you doing that? A body is lying there, someone's calling for help, you're rushing with water, and you're suddenly stopped by a trifle like clearing shards out of the window frame?"

"Well, yes. I'm so meticulous that I had to clean it up on the spot."

"Ma'am," says the judge placatingly, "if you showed remorse and told the truth, it would be a mitigating circumstance. You could get yourself a lawyer and it would be easier to defend you!"

"I don't need a lawyer," she replies, "because I don't feel I'm guilty. If you're such a psychologist, then you can prove to the court that I'm a criminal."

A journalist for *Słowo Polskie* writes: "As she makes her statement, she sets her jaw and maintains the tone she's struck since the very start. When they lay out the material evidence for her, her whole face turns crimson down to the neck, but she smiles derisively and denies everything."

IT CAN'T BE HER

Lwów, Sunday, February 7, 1932

Judge Zdzisław Kulczycki orders Warden Majewski of Brygidki Prison to release Engineer Zaremba. The investigation into him as a suspect has been closed for lack of evidence.

"It was understood that I had fallen victim to an atrocious blunder," noted Zaremba.

Early the next morning, on February 7, 1932, the guards lead him to the prison office. There, Inspector Raczyński, the prison warden's deputy, personally bids him farewell.

"I've ordered them to take you out by the side gate because folks have been swarming around at the main one since this morning," he tells Zaremba. He explains to him that his time in prison had made him a very well-known and popular person in Poland.

"You could make a pile of money on articles about yourself," he says.

The journalists aren't so easily fooled. When the side gate of the prison opens for Zaremba at ten o'clock, after five weeks in detention, there's already a small group of the most tenacious newshounds standing on the other side.

"I have to go to the cemetery, to my daughter's grave," Zaremba informs them.

"We understand," is their friendly reply. "We'll drive you there."

The news cars park at the very gate the police were guarding not long ago. A trampled path leads to Lusia's grave. Dry flowers and wilted wreaths protrude from the snow. Zaremba kneels.

"You see, Lusia," he whispers to himself, "strangers were allowed to pay their respects, but Tineczek [her nickname for him] couldn't say goodbye, because he was being kept in jail."

"My arrest was enough to plunge me into a mire of slander. My beloved Lwów stripped me of respect on the strength of newspaper rumors," he wrote.

So he doesn't read many newspapers. Staś screens the mail for letters full of venom and threats.

Their senders offer heartfelt wishes: that he should sit in the dock beside Gorgonowa, that he should be struck dead and dangle from a noose.

He can't go out on the street. Wherever he appears, fingers point at him, crowds cluster around him. Everywhere he hears behind his back: "That's Zaremba, Zaremba, Zaremba."

"I feel as though a motorman, having spotted me somewhere at a bend in the road, will forget his streetcar and turn onto the wrong line, that a carriage driver will drop the reins from his hands, that a driver will pull up onto the sidewalk to get a look at me."

For a long time, Zaremba can't believe his partner's guilt. During his first interrogation in Lwów, he quails when he learns that she is probably the one who killed his daughter.

"It can't be her," he tries to persuade Frankiewicz and Respond.

Then they calmly and logically explain to him that it couldn't be anyone else.

"No one but her," they say. "Because you didn't murder your daughter, did you? And her brother didn't kill his sister. And the third member of the household, on whom the circumstantial evidence focused, forming a chain of evidence, was Gorgonowa."

"Think of it this way," Frankiewicz and Respond tell him, "an unknown murderer would have fled in fear, not gone through the trouble of hiding [the weapon] in the pool."

They tell him about the little footprints leading from the large porch to the small one, right up to the door of her bedroom, about the fur coat with traces of feces, about the handkerchief found in the basement, and about Staś waking up in the middle of the night and the dark blur in the foyer that didn't answer when he called out, "Lusia!"

When they finish their questioning, Zaremba gives in to the pressure of their suggestions. He asks to add one final sentence to his statement:

"Based on the evidence gathered by the office conducting the investigation, I believe the perpetrator of the murder is Margarita Emilia Gorgonowa; but I did not participate, either before or after the fact, and it never even occurred to me that such a thing could transpire."

He writes in his book:

> I remember well that moment when her name was mentioned as that of the culprit, it was like a bolt of lightning within me. I felt terror. I didn't immediately have a flash of revelation. I didn't immediately recall Gorgonowa's eyes, so often burning with anger, which I found so strange, at the poor girl. Nor did I immediately recall the queer terror that filled Staś's eyes from the moment of that terrible discovery, eyes that had seen something that night, that were telling me some horrible truth that his mouth—my young boy's, my son's—felt unable to entrust to his father, his baby sister Romusia's father.
>
> Now it was becoming clear to me that my boy—awakened in the night, surprised by the whining of

the dog, terrified that the figure he spotted in the foyer did not answer back—had in fact seen Gorgonowa.

Henryk Mikołaj Zaremba, of the Dęboróg coat of arms, was born
in Nowy Sącz on September 10, 1883, the son of Bolesław and Stefania, née Strowska. After his father's death, he escaped poverty and,
with support from his uncle, graduated from the Industrial College
in Kraków (Faculty of Architecture and Construction) in 1904. After his studies, he went to work in Lwów, where, since 1911, he's had
his own architecture and construction studio, ZAREMBA & CO. He
designs important buildings in Lwów: the pavilion of the Eastern
Market, two clinics, the Polish Emigrants' Home, a lawyer's cham-
bers, and the Palace of Sport; he oversees the expansion of the main
train station, the largest and, in the eyes of Lwów's citizens, the most
beautiful in Poland.

He is chair of the Chamber of Builders and the Union of Visual
Artists, secretary of the Architects' Club and the Art Council, man-
ager of the Polish Building Society, and he sits on the board of the
Construction Bank.

In 1912, he marries Elżbieta Stenzel, daughter of a senior inspector on the Warsaw–Vienna railroad. Part of her dowry is the villa in
Brzuchowice.

In 1914, Lusia is born—and in 1917, Staś.

After their wedding, his wife Elżbieta starts behaving strangely.
She forgets important things, doesn't always know who she is, and
fails to recognize her loved ones, sometimes even her own children.
She rises before dawn and wanders the house with a little feather
duster, brushing off nonexistent dirt. In 1923, she's sent to a closed
facility for the mentally ill in Kulparków, outside the city.

Zaremba writes: "I was the forty-year-old widower of a wife buried alive in a hospital, the father of two children—Lusia was ten
years old, Staś was six. I thought the children—whom I wanted to

DID THIS HAND KILL?

place in the countryside, in Brzuchowice—would benefit greatly from a nursemaid."

In summer 1924, his friend Mrs. Baltinowa, a major's wife, tells him: "You need to get a nursemaid for your children who will also run the household."

And before he can say anything, she adds:

"I've just come across the right person. Kind, lively, cheerful, energetic, thrifty, clever. Besides, she's in a tough situation, I'd very much like to lend her a helping hand."

FROM DALMATIA TO POLAND

In March 1933, she tells the psychiatrists testing her sanity how she came from distant Dalmatia to Poland.

She doesn't remember her father. She was born two months before he died. Her mother said he was a doctor. At the age of four, her mother hands her over to an uncle to raise her—and at the age of six, she's moved to an orphanage run by the White Sisters in Sarajevo. She will graduate from the convent's elementary school.

After war breaks out in 1914, the nuns close down the convent and send the children home. Little Rita returns to her family. Her mother, stepfather, and stepsiblings live on the island of Zlarin, not far from the main town of Šibenik.

A regiment of the Austro-Hungarian Army is stationed in that city. Erwin Gorgon is a telegraph operator there. They meet when he takes a boat to the island for the christening of her mother's latest child.

Rita is fifteen when she marries Erwin Gorgon, nine years her senior, in Šibenik on September 2, 1916. They live for a few months with Rita's mother. Then he is transferred to a signal unit in Tribunj.

In September 1917, their only child is born—Erwinek. Three months later, her husband brings her and the baby to Lwów, while he himself returns to the front.

Rita moves in with her in-laws at 21 Wąska Street in Zamarstynów district, where the Gorgons own the largest mustard factory in Galicia.

At this time, Lwów is a dangerous city. The Poles are demanding independence, while the Austrians offer only repression and imprisonment. At the end of 1918, the Poles and Ukrainians begin a bloody struggle for the city. There is no gas, water, or electricity. Hunger and inflation rage.

In late 1918, Erwin Gorgon returns from the war. He is cold and unapproachable, and he immediately leaves Lwów to work for the Provincial Administration in Kamieniec Podolski, over two hundred kilometers away. He rarely visits his wife. ("We loved each other very much, but he suffered from a disease that prevented us from having marital relations, and we had to separate.")

In 1921, Gorgon reveals his greatest secret to her. During the war he caught syphilis from the wife of a certain admiral. So he's leaving for the United States, but he promises that once he's recovered a little, set himself up, gotten on his feet, he'll send for her and baby Erwinek.

She stays behind with his family.

Her later fate we learn from letters she sends to her husband in the U.S. (Erwin Gorgon forwarded them to the court from across the Atlantic. During the trial in Lwów, they were leaked, and their contents ended up on the front pages of the tabloids.) "My dearest," writes Rita in dark-blue ink, pressing hard on the nib:

> When your father burst into the room with his knife, telling me to get out of his house and that there was nothing for me there, I left so awash in tears I could barely walk out the door. Living conditions here are very hard and people from every branch of employment have been laid off. Thousands are on a slippery

path and can't cope. And what about me, without any skills or anyone? I got a job in a candy store [Mascotte on Legiony Street] as a cashier and within three months I had to put down a thousand-złoty deposit. Where was I meant to get that?

I got a room with a certain bricklayer on Rzeźbiarska Street, but I was twenty złotys short and, since I couldn't pay him, I not only had to move out, but he kept my things. Everything fell through. Until an old Jewish woman took pity on me and offered me room and board for two months until I got a job.

I wouldn't rely on your parents, who've caused my misfortune. They wouldn't let me see my child because I'm poor.

I missed him so much my heart was breaking, and I wanted to see him, even from a distance. And once in winter I snuck like a villain into the alley by the window. I don't know who saw me, but the Old Man came running out and I had to flee like a thief to avoid hearing the horrible epithets with which he abused me. And, my soul and body broken on that winter night, I roamed the park until morning, so crushed by unhappiness that I didn't feel hunger or cold.

Curse the Old Man for making our child an orphan. For the harm he's done to me, for wasting our happiness and our life. May God avenge our suffering. He's got one foot in the grave. Curse him.

THE INDICTMENT

Lwów, Friday, February 19, 1932

Prosecutor Alfred Laniewski files the charges against Margarita Emilia Gorgonowa. (In late January 1932, he replaced Junior Prosecutor Emil Krynicki.) Forty-two-year-old Laniewski is the District Deputy Prosecutor, a former trial judge from nearby Szczerzec and an ace prosecutor in Lwów. He led the sensational trial for the bomb attack on President Wojciechowski in 1924. He quickly realized that, when it came to the Gorgonowa case, everything else would pale in comparison.

He wrote in his memoirs: "I joined [the case] with the greatest zeal, the greatest circumspection, and complete ardor. I immediately sensed the case would not run a normal course, that in it we would have to overcome extraordinary hurdles, that each step, each decision would have to be considered, analyzed, and probed a hundred times."

Prosecutor Laniewski is opposed to a summary judgment. He knows the material evidence is not nearly as rich, strong, and incontrovertible as the press would have it. He believes the case will have to be solved using standard procedure:

> I could see clear as day how this case would run, psychologically. I knew every step, even the slightest, taken

in the investigation would be used against us and at times even overturned. I knew as we examined that we could not overlook even the tiniest circumstance *pro* or *contra*. The task was to show in a strong and decisive fashion how the thing had actually occurred.

When he files the charges against Gorgonowa, he must realize the evidence is weak and will be questioned in court. He has his work cut out for him because the defendant will not confess.

The whole indictment rests on the testimony of a fourteen-year-old boy who has an antagonistic relationship with the defendant. The defense will surely want to use this to undermine his statements, and justifiably so. After all, the boy waited a long while before telling anyone what he saw in the foyer that night, and then he wasn't sure, and only a few hours later did it dawn on him that it was the Lady.

Laniewski must have had doubts. But he does not waver. Based on sections 134 and 135 of the Penal Code of 1852, introduced under Austrian rule and at this time still in force in Lwów, he charges Rita Gorgonowa with the murder of Elżbieta Zarembianka. This means there is only one possible punishment if she is found guilty—execution.

The indictment Laniewski writes is colorful but drawn in broad strokes, telling the story of Rita Gorgonowa, a lost emigrant from Yugoslavia, in search of help, ending up in the hands of a decent, older man from Brzuchowice. He takes her in as a nanny for his children but is too weak to resist her charms. She wraps him around her little finger and subdues him. His daughter, who wants to free her father from the arms of this usurper, becomes Gorgonowa's greatest enemy, the cause of her misfortune, an obstacle in her happy life with the gentleman from Brzuchowice. The girl is so successful that her father breaks off his relationship with his partner, which for Rita means ruin: less-favorable living conditions, not being able to keep her head above water.

In Laniewski's opinion, this was the primary motive for the murder.

"A string of unshakeable evidence has encircled the Defendant in an irrefutable ring of logic, revealing her as the perpetrator of this act," he writes in the indictment.

Yet the material evidence the prosecutor evokes is rather shallow: Apart from Staś Zaremba's murky statements, the indictment is stitched together from fragmentary circumstantial evidence, nothing strong and concrete.

Prosecutor Laniewski does his best to ignore this fact: "The work performed has been masterful, filigree, very precise," he says reassuringly. "Every item has been considered in numerous meetings and conferences, in a comprehensive manner. We have sought out the weaker angles of every individual conception, accepting them only when these weaker angles could be eliminated."

RITA'S NEW LIFE

At first, Rita lives on what Erwin sends from America, but it's not enough for her to support herself. When that, too, is cut off, her husband does not respond to her pleading letters.

No one knows where he is, what he's doing, whether he's alive at all. Contradictory news makes it to Lwów: that he's a captain on a ship, or that he spends whole days lying in an opium den. That he's living in Chicago, or maybe in New York. That he's alive. That he's dead.

It's not easy to find work in Lwów, especially for someone with no skills. Rita signs up for a nursing course with the well-known pediatrician Professor Franciszek Groër. He offers his graduates well-paid jobs in the pediatric clinic he runs. Rita has to drop out because she doesn't have any money. Instead of working at a hospital, she ends up at the high-class Mascotte candy store at 1 Legiony Street. In April 1924, an acquaintance of hers, Mrs. Baltinowa, tells her that a well-known Lwów architect might help her find an appropriate position. Henryk Zaremba comes to meet her at the candy store on Legiony and offers her a job. He says for the moment there are no positions in his office, but she should wait for one and, in the meantime, look after his children.

"Her face was kind, very handsome, though not enchanting"—Zaremba recalls of that first meeting. "I did not sense in this thirty-three-year-old woman any kind of demonic seductress who would make my blood boil and set my desires raging."

Zaremba at the time was a bald, wrinkled man eighteen years her senior. At that point, there was no question of love—just of looking after Staś and Lusia. Their mother had recently been sent to the psychiatric clinic in Kulparków, and he was struggling to keep up with work, the children, the house, and the servants.

Zaremba writes of Rita: "She was abandoned, she had no one. She married very well, but fortune had deserted her"—this was all he knew of her at the time. He offered a helping hand to rescue this beautiful stranger. Without requiring references, he offered her a job as a nanny in Brzuchowice. Rita would move in with Lusia and Staś, and he would come to visit only on Sundays.

Gorgonowa: "I hesitated about staying in Zaremba's home. I told him that by entering his house I would burn the bridge with my husband, to whom I would be unable to return. Then he answered that he would do his best to divorce his wife, and I would be the mother of his children."

"Her laugh filled the garden on that very first Sunday," writes Zaremba. "She conquered the hearts of my little ones. They took to her immediately. The children, hitherto shabby, began to look cleaner. The positive impression she made grew week by week, month by month."

He started visiting more often. With each trip, he liked her more. She was less and less a nursemaid, and more and more the Lady of the House.

One afternoon, he was alone in his architectural studio when she turned up unexpectedly.

"I looked at that laughing face of hers. Into those eyes, gazing brightly, confidently, calmly. [...] Since she had come on her own, I had to appreciate what she was offering," he thought, and invited the governess to his Lwów apartment for the night.

"I felt comfortable with Gorgonowa," he writes in his memoirs.

> I surrendered to the wave, or rather I was riding in a boat with my hand off the tiller, while she sat at the helm and gave that boat its direction. From a modest store clerk, she grew in her dreams into the landlady of the Brzuchowice villa, with the title of spouse to a man who, when all is said and done, has a respectable name and wealth.
>
> Our relationship grew more intimate, trusting, tender. [. . .] I no longer visited my country cottage merely as a father who missed his children. There was someone who, so I thought, was awaiting me with open arms. And by now I wanted something more than those tender embraces, which were still discreet in Brzuchowice. I wanted her arms to open wide and hug tight only for me. [. . .]
>
> We were walking down Szczepańska Street in Kraków. In the distance were the towers of St. Mary's Basilica. And suddenly the thought flashed through my mind: "What if we bound ourselves together with a vow?" (We could not legally belong to one another—neither one divorced.)
>
> I suggested:
>
> "Rita, what if we went into that church and there, before the altar in the face of God, without witnesses, we swore to one another faithful love—forever?"
>
> She stopped, stunned. Then she shook with laughter:

"And what if later on someone else catches my fancy?" [...]

I felt ice in my bones. [...] I did not hold it against her, she didn't want to join me in a vow. [...] She was a nanny and a mistress of the house, who could leave me at any moment. [...]

I introduced her to acquaintances as "my lady," and that was sufficient for them to give "my lady" her due. [...] In the village [...] people were convinced Gorgonowa was my wife. I did not protest at their misapprehension, for why should I have? [...]

IN THE PALACE OF JUSTICE

Lwów, Monday, April 25, 1932–Saturday, May 14, 1932

At the top: "Catalog number VII 2K 11/32." Below: "on the criminal case of Margarita Gorgonowa under section 134 of the criminal code." At the very bottom, scrawled in red ink, the signature of the trial's presiding judge, Jan Antoniewicz, plus the stamp of the court.

There's a battle in Lwów for every last ticket to the trial. There are thousands of takers, but the presiding judge can only issue 250 a day. He must share them out among journalists, judges, prosecutors, lawyers, and thousands of ordinary people who wish to see Gorgonowa up close.

"All of Lwów's judges, prosecutors, and even bailiffs were hounded by persons known and unknown for tickets," writes Prosecutor Alfred Laniewski. "They used every variety of subterfuge, patronage, or manipulation to get into the courtroom. People who hitherto had had nothing to do with the press apart from buying or borrowing newspapers every day became 'journalists' to get their hands on a press pass."

On Batory Street, the most important thoroughfare in the formerly suburban Halickie district, the police remove groups of gawkers trying to sneak into the Palace of Justice, which resembles an antique temple.

Those who have tickets line up by seven in the morning, two hours before the trial, to make sure they get in.

"Others stood out on the street by the gray wall of the building," writes Laniewski, "as if hoping those walls might by some miracle lift the veil on the secret they so badly craved to know, tell them at least a particle of everything that would soon happen in there. Everyone was driven by lust for sensation, lust for chills and thrills to serve at least as a substitute for that awful night before New Year's Eve, lust for seeing the people who had found themselves at the scene of the crime."

"What we witnessed yesterday on Batory Street was unlike anything hitherto seen in the history of the Lwów judiciary," writes *Gazeta Poranna*.

Courtroom 1. The largest in the Palace of Justice, upstairs, above the main entrance. Large windows look out over Batory Street. A crowd will wait here outside the door until the final day of the trial.

The first thing that catches the eye is the large iron bed to the left of the defense table. The bed has been made, as if someone were just about to lie down in it. Except the sheets are heavily stained with steel-gray and claret-colored spots.

Scattered around near the judges' bench are small wooden tables, holding the most important pieces of material evidence: an ice-axe, a candlestick, a nightgown, a brassiere, a handkerchief.

There are no special boxes for journalists. They sit in the first row of the gallery, with the ordinary public behind them.

"Faces young and old, beautiful and ugly, men and women. (The latter absolutely predominated.) These faces were flushed, in part due to the heat in the room, in part due to the general excitement," writes Laniewski.

Before nine, the journalists' seats are filling up. There are news photographers and sketch artists.

Just behind the barrier for the gallery, two stenographers sit at a small table. They work for *Ilustrowany Kurier Codzienny*, which has also sent their judicial reporter to the trial. They are to take transcription in turns. As one types up his notes, the other will copy down everything in the courtroom so that no word is lost, no comma, no period.

Couriers will collect the typescripts, then dictate them by telephone to typists on duty at the paper's headquarters in Kraków, on the corner of Starowiślna and Wielopole Streets. This is editor-in-chief Marian Dąbrowski's idea for getting the better of the competition. All the newspapers have reports from the trial, but only *Ilustrowany Kurier Codzienny* has the full text: word for word. (The reports are so precise that later the Supreme Court will use clippings from the newspaper equally alongside the trial minutes.)

Starting on Monday, April 25, 1932, every day, seven days a week, *Ilustrowany Kurier Codzienny* publishes four- or five-page reports from Lwów.

At 9:05, Bailiff Biłobran enters the courtroom and gives everyone the signal to rise.

Through the back doors just behind the judge's bench, the penal tribunal enters: Presiding Judge Jan Antoniewicz (at this time Vice-Chairman of the District Court in Lwów), and Judges Robert Tertil and Sylwester Łyczkowski.

"Seasoned, experienced judges. Wise and good people," Laniewski writes of them.

At the defense table, sitting alone, is a tall, heavy, and nearly bald forty-year-old man with a partial comb-over. This is the lawyer Maurycy Axer, a graduate of the Law Faculty of Lwów University, a former lieutenant in the Austro-Hungarian horse artillery (in which he spent nearly four years on the Russian, Italian, and Albanian fronts during the Great War), the best speaker of the Bar in Lwów. Since 1919 he has run a practice at 4a Fredro Street, specializing in criminal and political cases. But only now is his name on the lips of everyone in Poland, with the most important newspapers seeking interviews.

"If I have taken on this case, I wish for truth to triumph," he tells *Express Wieczorny Ilustrowany*. "I believe in my client's innocence. Otherwise I would have long ago abandoned her defense, which has inflicted on me serious costs and losses."

(He already knows this is the most important case of his career. People will ask him about it for the rest of his life, until his final journey by cargo train from Lwów to the death camp in Bełżec in 1942.)

"He impressed me," recalls Laniewski. "He went manfully into a terrible battle. He knew what awaited him. He went prepared for any sacrifice, of which he later bore so many in this case. Prepared to make every effort. (It is said he cared only for satisfying his ambition. Perhaps so, but a noble ambition it was.)"

All that remains is for Presiding Judge Antoniewicz to randomly select a twelve-person jury and then the trial will be underway. (In accordance with the Austrian criminal procedure still in force, this will be a trial by jury, with the judges determining only the sentence.)

For the security of the trial, Gorgonowa is transferred to a gloomy jail that stands in the courtyard of the Palace of Justice, inside a former Carmelite convent. This means the defendant will not have to be transported to her trial through the whole city, putting her at risk of lynching. She will be brought into the courtroom via a special corridor connecting the jail with the courthouse.

At 9:15 she enters the room under guard.

She is wearing a black, sealskin fur coat, a small green cap, patent leather shoes, and black gloves, which she does not remove for the whole trial. She will use them to hide her face from the nosy reporters trying to immortalize the tears glistening in her eyes.

"She has nothing of the charm that men once found irresistible. Her face is ruined. She looks old, she is broken and agitated. She surely knows she is breathing an atmosphere bereft of all sympathy and compassion," reports *Tajny Detektyw*.

She sits in a chair facing the judges' bench, her back to the public gallery so they cannot see her face.

Reporting Clerk Janowski reads the indictment in a clear and sonorous voice. He could do it in a whisper and still he'd be heard in every corner of the jam-packed courtroom because everyone is incredibly focused and quiet. Gorgonowa listens too. She sits motionless, staring at the reporting clerk. She sniffles. Sometimes her tears grow more copious.

She rises, dejected.

"I was born on March seventh, 1901, in Oćestovo, I am married, I have two children: one with Gorgon, the other with Zaremba," she begins quietly. "My religion is Greek Catholic. My husband is named Erwin, he's living in America. I don't know his occupation, and I only have an elementary school education."

She speaks tentatively. It seems like she isn't defending herself.

She will continue her statements sitting down, on her doctor's recommendation.

Suddenly her voice sounds sure and resonant. The hands that a moment ago nervously pinched at her thighs now make lively gestures. With each moment she grows stronger.

She does not admit guilt. She deplores the horrific course of events. For each charge of the indictment she has a ready answer.

She says she never felt hatred for Lusia. It's a lie that she allegedly threatened the girl. She didn't need to kill anyone because she knew that Zaremba would soon end their relationship, and she accepted her fate. The shadow Staś Zaremba spotted in the foyer couldn't have been her, she was still sleeping at the time; the footprints in the snow don't prove anything. It's not even certain they belonged to her, and if they did, well, after all, she left the house to call the doctor. She had nothing to do with the ice-axe, and she left the bloody handkerchief in the cellar a few days before the incident, when she cut her finger down there. She didn't change her nightgown nor burn it. She went to sleep in a white one and got up in a white one. The witnesses must have gotten something wrong. Blood on her sleeve? The analysis was wrong: it must have been paint.

She defends herself fiercely, plausibly, with enormous assertiveness and even insolence. Her story forms a relatively logical whole.

She admits that many details weigh against her, yet all the more forcefully she asserts her innocence.

"She defends herself with the might of her instinct," the papers write of her.

"Not very sympathetic. As if she'd come to court to quarrel," notes Prosecutor Laniewski. (By now he must know that the case is very difficult and could be a turning point in his career.)

His assessment of her is wrong. He need only read the reports of journalists seeing their subject for the first time. Until now, they only knew her from the accounts of bystanders and from rumors. They expected to encounter a demon, the incarnation of evil, but they found an intelligent, composed woman, who, despite her agitation, controls her every response, her every word.

"An absolutely intelligent and clever woman. Unbending and unmoved. Not heeding whether her declarations are logical or not, whether they find belief or they do not, if they align with or contradict the findings of the investigation. She stated them bravely, without stammering, with nerve," writes *Ilustrowany Kurier Codzienny* after the first day of the trial.

> Her voice—weak to start, who knows whether deliberately or unconsciously— gathered strength in the course of the questioning. She quickly attuned herself to her surroundings, to the atmosphere of the court-

room and from then on acted with complete control and confidence. Witnesses who are inconvenient to her become the objects of malicious and harsh barbs. She unflinchingly accused the investigative bodies of carelessness in their tests and procedures.

She explains what she can and denies what she cannot. These descriptions of the first day of the trial show amazement and surprise. Amazement that she did not break. Surprise that she bravely defends herself. Readers can't get enough.

WITNESS NUMBER ONE

Lwów, Tuesday, April 26, 1932

Everything matters: how she's dressed, how her hair is done, whether she walks confidently, whether she smiles, how she sits, where she looks. These details can be found every day in the newspapers.

So we know that on the second day of the trial—Tuesday, April 26, 1932—she is again wearing the sealskin fur, her cheeks are flushed, and she walks into the courtroom with an assured, even step. (She does not look at the hostile gallery.)

The evidentiary stage of the trial commences. Stanisław Zaremba—tall, slim, mature beyond his years (he is in fifth grade at High School no. 9 in Lwów)—takes the stand in athletic dress, raises his right hand over a cross and repeats after Presiding Judge Antoniewicz in a trembling voice:

"I swear to Almighty and Omniscient God that I will tell the honest truth, concealing nothing that is known to me. So help me God."

He begins timidly, smiling nervously.

He doesn't remember when his mother was committed to the mental hospital, but he does remember he was a little boy when he lost her, and that at that time they lived on Zielona Street in Lwów. Then *she* came. She was supposed to run the household, cook and clean, but she took his mother's place at his father's side.

The court asks whether he and Lusia knew that his father's relationship with the defendant was not the typical one with a housekeeper.

"It hurt us that our mama was sick, still alive, that Papa could divorce Mama to marry her."

"Did you often quarrel?" asks the court.

"In recent times, very often," says the witness accusingly. "She was even prejudiced against me, for any silly mistake she called me stupid, an idiot."

And the boy's trembling voice turns into a sob. He sniffles, and the courtroom is moved. Ladies pull white handkerchiefs from their purses and also whimper.

"Staś, please collect yourself," Judge Antoniewicz appeals gently. "A fifteen-year-old boy should be manly."

Staś's tale of the suffering felt by children deprived of a mother's love moves the listeners, and the boy's tears arouse compassion. He is winning their sympathy.

The courtroom is on his side as the most important moment of the trial takes place, as the teenager decides the life or death of the woman who raised him.

He testifies confidently. How the dog's barking awakened him, how he noticed a figure between the piano and the Christmas tree, how he called out "Lusia!" and it wasn't her standing there, and how he then saw a shadow slipping down the porch stairs on the left.

"I recognized her by her hair and her profile," he says assuredly, but, giving himself cover, adds: "At first, it didn't even register in my mind because I was so upset, though later I realized it was clearly her."

Mr. Axer presses the witness:

"Did you first notice her features and then become aware it was the defendant, or did you know right away that it was her?"

"I saw her features but only became aware it was her an hour and a half later."

"When you became aware of it, where were you at the time?"

"At that point I was in the dining room. The outpost commander had arrived. And that was later. Maybe two hours!"

"Why didn't you say so right away?"

"There was no time."

When Henryk Zaremba testifies after a recess, he cries as well. His mustache shaved, his hair gray, his suit black, in mourning for his daughter.

He sobs as he recalls how he ran into his murdered little girl's room and touched her still-warm hand, all the while clinging to hope. But that soon deserted him.

The ladies in the room pull out their handkerchiefs again as he speaks of holding his child's hand for the last time.

But his testimony adds little to solving Lusia's murder.

The last witness that day is Maria Lucht (the wife of one of the Zarembas' former gardeners) and of her testimony, only one sentence is worth remembering: "Once Gorgonowa told me she'd sooner shoot Zaremba than leave his house."

THE KILLER WAS SOMEONE IN THE HOUSE

Lwów, Wednesday, April 27, 1932

For weeks, there has been much talk of a witness who is meant to change the course of the trial.

His appearance has long been hinted at by Prosecutor Laniewski. He says that together they will demonstrate Gorgonowa's limitless hatred for Lusia.

Today this mysterious witness is meant to finally sink her, pin her down, drive a stake through her heart so she can't rise again. Leave no one with any doubt about Gorgonowa's intentions or her guilt. He is an ace up the prosecutor's sleeve.

But before this witness takes the stand, into Courtroom 1 comes forty-five-year-old Dr. Ludwik Csala, Zaremba's neighbor. He was the first in the architect's villa to say that Lusia must have been murdered by a member of the household.

Now he testifies how he came to realize that:

"I was thinking over how the attacker could have snuck into the villa. I noticed the door from the porch into the hall had the bolt unlocked. Then I remarked that, without damaging the frame, it could only be unlocked from the inside. Then the defendant pointed out the bandit could have come in through the window, and reminded Zaremba that, after all, he had seen an open window in Lusia's room.

But opening the window from outside without damaging the glass was also impossible. All of that led me to suspect the culprit was already inside the house."

After Csala, the thirty-one-year-old gardener Józef Kamiński takes the stand. (He doesn't know that in a moment he will go from witness to prime suspect—that, until the end of his life, he will never escape these suspicions. For the next fifty years, he will struggle in vain to clear his name.)

Before he begins to testify, Axer asks the court to swear the witness in.

"Because he also stands under suspicion of murdering Lusia," he proclaims to the shocked judges. The courtroom breaks out in commotion, the prosecutor leaps to his feet.

"Not a single comma in the files implicates him," protests Laniewski, as if blindsided by the line of defense newly unfurling before his eyes.

Axer seeks to convince the court that Lusia's murder could not conceivably have been committed by a woman, because none would be able to deal such powerful, skull-smashing blows.

He sows doubts among the journalists in the court hallways, explaining that in the history of criminology there has never been a case of a woman deflowered by another woman.

"It is difficult to conclude," he says, "that in the mind of even a refined murderess, the thought would occur to perform so atrocious an act only to deflect suspicion and lend the crime the characteristics of a sexual murder. How unshakably cold-blooded would Gorgonowa need to be to allow herself to disgrace the body of a dying victim?"

For this line of defense to hold water, Axer had to locate a murderer other than Gorgonowa, and groundskeeper Kamiński—surly, unsympathetic, taciturn—fit the bill fantastically. In particular because just after the murder, one of the many rumors, hypotheses, and questions circulating was, "Couldn't it be the gardener?" Axer knows that there is absolutely no way of proving it, but he can undermine facts that are being taken as true. It's not a professional judge deciding who's guilty, but twelve random people the court selected by lottery.

Kamiński's testimony, like that of his wife Rozalia, doesn't add much to the case—apart from one tiny detail. Kamiński claims that on the night of the crime, Staś told him the mysterious apparition was the Lady. (Young Zaremba doesn't remember this.)

The next witness, the surprise one, is named Antoni Halemba. He's thirty-one years old and a private investigator in Tarnowskie Góry, near Katowice. He is the witness everyone has been waiting for. A commotion goes up the moment he walks into the courtroom, but it dies down once he begins testifying.

He speaks confidently, with verve, and a slight German accent.

Last fall he received a mysterious letter. Inside the envelope were one hundred złotys, a request to come to Lwów, and instructions that, just before his train pulled into the station, he should wave a white handkerchief out the window. Two unfamiliar women approached him on the platform and drove him to a house. There he was offered vodka and a job. He was to seduce a girl and provide irrefutable evidence that he had. He didn't accept, he says, because the proposal was immoral.

He only realized in January that it was Gorgonowa who tried to hire him, after he saw her picture in *Tajny Detektyw*. He wrote to the investigating judge because he realized she'd meant to use him as a tool to shame Lusia and undermine trust in her.

The court orders Halemba to approach the stand and inspect Gorgonowa from close-up. He has no doubts. He says she is the one who hired him.

Halemba's testimony doesn't help solve Lusia's mysterious death, but it does overturn the whole masterfully constructed line of defense: if the defendant tried something like this scheme to shame the girl, she is capable of anything.

Axer tries to cast doubt on the prosecution's witnesses. With this one that's not hard because Halemba doesn't remember a single detail of his visit to Lwów. He doesn't know when he arrived, on which street the house he'd visited was located, or even what play he saw at the theater.

Stony-faced, the defense asks the witness a final question:

"How long," inquires Axer with utmost politeness, "did you spend in a lunatic asylum?"

The witness replies equally politely:

"Two years." He specifies: "In 1925 and '26."

But Halemba's answer renders his testimony worthless. Soon it's discovered that the private investigator has himself been repeatedly tried for fraud, extortion, and violence. A year and a half later, in October 1933, he will be sentenced to three years in prison for spying for Germany.

Next to testify is Józef Nuckowski, commander of the police station in Rzęsna Polska, who was alerted to the murder by the police in Lwów. He reached the villa at 3:20 A.M. and was the first police officer there. He was the one who found Gorgonowa's wet, bloody handkerchief in the cellar, and also the one whom Staś told about the figure slightly taller than his sister he saw in the night. (At the time the boy didn't mention she looked like Gorgonowa.)

Following him is thirty-five-year-old Sergeant Stanisław Trela from the nearby military police station, who was the first government official to arrive at the scene of the crime. In search of the murderer, he followed the footprints in the snow, but the trail broke off by the small porch. He found no footprints by the wall surrounding the villa. He had also started to suspect that it was a member of the household who killed Lusia.

EXAMINING THE SERVANTS

Lwów, Thursday, April 28, 1932

Far from subsiding, interest in the trial grows daily.

Tajny Detektyw explains the phenomenon:

> The mystery of the fascination this trial elicits lies in its extraordinary nature. Here, it's not important, eye-catching events but trifles, tiny trifles, that take on significance, determine life and death, freedom or imprisonment. A shadow of a figure, a key, a broken windowpane, a whiff of kerosene, a vanished night-gown, a few hairs from a fur coat, drops of blood, shards of glass, even a candle-stub—all join together in a tangle of details, mysteriously intriguing.
>
> Here imagination can run wild, as in a dream, as in a novel, as at the cinema.
>
> Those listening to the proceedings, and also those reading about it, are in thrall to this riddle of trifles. To solve these is to solve the mystery of the crime Journalists are calling today's proceedings an examination of the housekeeping office, because it will mostly be staff.

First up is Bronisława Beckerówna (who worked for Zaremba until August 1931):

"The defendant said to Zaremba: 'You old swine, get your bastards out of here or I'll kill them.'"

Olga Jezierska (September–October 1931):

"Gorgonowa always said about Lusia: 'That rascal, that monkey, may she drop dead, God damn her.' She said everything was Lusia's fault, that she was getting in her way and encouraging her father to break things off with her."

Marcelina Tobiaszówna (in Brzuchowice up until Zaremba's arrest):

"Gorgonowa resented Lusia for wanting her and Zaremba to split up."

Helena Płocka (a friend of Zarembianka's from Olga Filippi High School):

"Her stepmother used to threaten Lusia that she'd poison her and shoot her."

Piotr Kiszakiewicz (a close friend of Zaremba's):

"Gorgonowa complained that Lusia didn't let her live with Zaremba. That she spread rumors and stole letters."

Włodzimierz Bielecki (a painter and friend of Zaremba's):

"Zarembianka kept saying she'd like her father's relationship with the defendant to be broken off. She was afraid the defendant would poison her."

The courtroom hosts a parade of young and old, rich and poor, women and men, doctors, engineers, students, society women, and unemployed men. All of them say the same thing: that Rita was a wicked stepmother and threatened Zarembianka's life.

"The women following their hearts are all against her," notes *Ilustrowany Kurier Codzienny*.

How does Rita respond to these accusations?

She brushes them off with silence. Or laughter, leading the gallery to believe that the entire world is against her.

"Gorgonowa's behavior in the courtroom is considerably remarkable," writes *Tajny Detektyw*.

> Anyone seeking to peer through the mask of her face into the depths of her soul would soon find themselves at a loss. For seven hours a day she sits almost motionless in her chair, stonily calm. This even gains her a certain sympathy from the gallery. But if she suddenly rises, if she begins to speak, her voice, naturally fairly sweet, repels everyone with some ill-hidden note of passion. We are led to believe that in the domestic sphere, when something did not go as she would like, she knew how to use a loud quarrel to get her way. The defense counsel realizes the malign impression that the accused's voice inadvertently makes. He only reluctantly allows her to speak, and if she starts up, he always gives a hand signal to stop.

At 1:55 P.M., Presiding Judge Antoniewicz calls a recess. The proceedings will continue in Brzuchowice.

At 5 P.M., a string of cars sets off from the front of the courthouse on Batory Street. At lightning speed, word goes around Lwów that the panel of judges and the defendant are on their way to Brzuchowice. People who didn't make it into the courtroom line up along the roadside, mainly women in headscarves. The crowds are visible in photographs of the site visit. If Rita can see through the grated windows of the prison van, she can see a mass of people shaking their fists, whistling and hurling insults.

On Marszałkowska Street in Brzuchowice, in front of the Zarembas' villa, the crowd grows so large that the police are needed to maintain order.

Inside, the High Commission examines the frame of the porch window in Rita's room. There's still a hole in it from the broken pane, and nails protrude from it. The panel of judges takes a seat at the table in the dining room as Staś Zaremba hops into the divan bed by the window.

And once again he wakes up, peers through the window, once again he cries "Lusia!" then goes up to the French door and knocks on the windowpane, behind which the High Commission has placed Rita. (On the court's orders, she is dressed in a brown fur coat and slippers.)

And then the boy once again implicates her:

"I recognized her as she was going out the half-open door into the yard," he assures them.

In Zaremba's bedroom, the commission watches him leap out of bed and race to Lusia's room; in Rita's bedroom, they observe how she smashed the glass, while in the garden, Sergeant Trela shows them on green grass where he saw footprints in the snow.

The commission inspects the cellar, the drained pool, and the cracked window in groundskeeper Kamiński's house where the police found bloody handprints.

But the press photographers are more interested in the defendant herself, who runs away from them, shielding her face with her hands.

"You've already got enough pictures in the magazines!" she shouts.

At 8 P.M., as it's getting dark, the commission leaves the villa in the convoy and continues all the way to the Lwów city limits.

Ilustrowany Kurier Codzienny writes that a five-thousand-strong group of women met them with sticks, batons, and stones, wanting to dish out justice to the child-killer. Gorgonowa's life was saved because the head of the prison convoy, warned of the danger, sped up the van to try to force his way through the blockade. At the sight of the speeding vehicle, the crowd parted and only pelted it with stones. All the prison van's windows were smashed, but the attempt to kill Gorgonowa was unsuccessful. No stone even grazed her.

SHE'S NOT TELLING THE TRUTH

Lwów, Friday, April 29, 1932

"The trial had entered its final act. The jurors had now been perfectly appraised of the extensive and complex factual material. This was evident from the questions they posed to individual witnesses via the presiding judge," wrote Prosecutor Laniewski in his memoir.

Today is the last day of questioning. The two most important witnesses will testify: the county chief of police, Senior Commissioner Józef Frankiewicz, and Aspirant Bolesław Respond. The former led the police investigation; the latter was one of the most important detectives.

When Frankiewicz reached the villa, Zaremba told him that a break-in and murder had been committed, but doubts started nagging at the commissioner's mind because an adult couldn't have squeezed through the window in Lusia's room.

He recounted how with each passing moment he grew increasingly convinced the murder was committed by a member of the household. He was put onto Gorgonowa's trail by the footprints in the snow and the bloody, wet handkerchief found in the basement. He brought it to her room and asked if it was her property. She confirmed it was.

"I must have lost it down there," she replied. Yet to Frankiewicz's mind, the handkerchief couldn't have been lost but must have been hidden on purpose, since it was balled up and concealed under a box of graphite.

Then he told Gorgonowa that all suspicions were aligned against her, so she should help them uncover the truth. She only tossed her head. She made no reply.

Zaremba was sitting at the table in the dining room. Frankiewicz told him about his misgivings toward Gorgonowa.

"Would you have suspected her after so many years living together?" asked Zaremba, amazed. He couldn't believe it.

Bolesław Respond questioned Staś three times. He was the first policeman whom the boy told that he recognized the mysterious figure as the Lady. The court must now attempt to establish whether Respond inadvertently suggested that answer to Staś himself.

"Absolutely not," protests Respond. "During the very first interview I got a hunch that Staś wanted to tell me something more, but didn't have the courage, as if he wanted to talk with his father first. He was nervous, near tears."

The boy mustered up the courage during the second interview.

"Then I asked Staś again," testifies Respond, "whether he had, in fact, recognized the figure. This time he informed me he recognized it as Gorgonowa, and when I asked why he hadn't said so before, he stated he'd been very nervous and hadn't known what he was saying."

Staś Zaremba revealed one more important detail to Respond. When he was going to sleep, he saw Rita lying in bed in a willow-green nightgown, and when the police arrived, she was in a white one. (This is a key piece of circumstantial evidence in the indictment, intended to confirm the thesis that Gorgonowa killed Lusia and then disposed of her own bloodstained nightgown. However, the police never found a willow-green nightgown.)

Respond points out one more particularly important piece of circumstantial evidence implicating Gorgonowa: her bloody handprint on the window of the gardener's house, which she knocked on that ill-fated night to wake him up. He recalls that in her statements Gorgonowa claimed she didn't approach Lusia's blood-covered body, and as soon as she entered the room she was sent out again to fetch Dr. Csala. Only after coming back did she go to the pool to get some water, and it was then that she cut her hand. But if that were so, she couldn't have gotten blood on the Kamińskis' windowpane because she knocked on it before she went to get water.

"That led us to believe she wasn't telling the truth," Respond explains to the judge. "She must have cut her hand before she went to get the doctor. The position of the putty and the direction of the glass shards indicated that she broke the pane from the outside."

"And you didn't notice the traces of blood on the gardener's window?" asks Axer, mockingly.

"No. It was only noticed on August eighth," replies Respond.

When Maurycy Axer is completely helpless in the face of witness testimony, he does his best to latch onto tiny inconsistencies, inaccuracies, oversights, absurdities, doubts, ridiculousnesses. So he asks Aspirant Respond about the blood on Kamiński's windowpane because he knows the police bungled it up. They only found the handprint a week later, once frost, snow, and rain had taken their toll, and little possibility remained of establishing the blood type. This could have been the crowning piece of evidence if not for the police's ineptitude.

This is how Axer implements the defense he's outlined for her. He intends to prove Rita Gorgonowa's innocence by two means. In case she's found guilty, he wants to do as much as he can to demonstrate that the court has overlooked a great deal of evidence. Therefore, each day of the trial he makes an enormous number of motions: to constantly call new witnesses, to make a new site visit, to administer psychiatric tests on the defendant and Staś. All to build a legal basis for an appeal. But that will only happen if the main line of defense fails. Axer is consistently trying to demonstrate that the crime in

Brzuchowice could not have been committed by a woman because it was a sexual murder, committed in a fit of lechery by a psychopathic male killer prowling the area around Lwów.

In photos of the trial, Maurycy Axer's black robe makes him look like a good-natured parish priest with the face of a Baroque angel and a bald head with a meticulous partial combover. Tall, fairly heavyset, with his chin held proudly high. He looks straight ahead, over the gallery of faces glaring at him in hostility. When he defends the accused too aggressively, the courtroom makes its displeasure known. It grumbles, rustles, creaks. But so far only one occasion has provoked shouts and stamping of feet, when Axer said directly:

"A woman could not have committed this crime."

After listening to today's testimony, the gallery thinks everything is settled. To them, the recent days' parade of witnesses has confirmed without question that Gorgonowa is guilty, that she was a bad caregiver who didn't look after the children she was entrusted with, that she insulted them, treated them like dirt, and threatened their lives. Admittedly, there is no strong, direct, decisive proof—but the circumstantial evidence strongly implicates her. They don't know why she doesn't admit her guilt and insists on denying everything.

Because even if everything isn't completely clear so far, tomorrow the expert witnesses will testify and dispel all doubts. They will finish what the ordinary witnesses could not.

The newspapers predict: "Science will have the last word in the evidentiary proceedings."

THE TURNING POINT

Lwów, Saturday, April 30, 1932

At 9 A.M., when Rita—in a light-colored summer coat—steps into the courtroom, nothing hints at the earthquake to come. On this day a great turnaround in the trial will take place, and the legend will be born—a legend alive to this day—of Rita Gorgonowa, the Polish Dreyfus.

But first, Dr. Karol Piro from the Institute of Forensic Medicine at Jan Kazimierz University in Lwów reads out the findings of his autopsy:

"On Lusia's head were three transverse wounds, four centimeters in size. The bones of her skull were exposed, the right side of her face was bruised, there were abrasions on the skin of her neck, her fingers were slightly wounded, her brain was inundated with blood. The cause of death was a fracture of the skull. The injury was caused by a blunt instrument. There are no traces of defense. That is a sign that the first blow was successful. Experts confirmed injury to the deceased's internal reproductive organs, inflicted postmortem or while dying. These were caused by the insertion of some solid object, probably fingers."

Presiding Judge Antoniewicz reads out the report from the examination of the defendant's hand:

"On the back of the left hand are four small, linear wounds, and on the forearm, just below the elbow, there are also several cuts to the skin. Traces of fecal matter were found on the defendant's body." Doctor Antoni Westfalewicz from the university's Institute of Forensic Chemistry delivers the results of the blood test and the traces of blood found in the villa.

He confirms that Rita Gorgonowa's blood is type O while Zarembianka's is type A. He reads off a lengthy list of items of evidence that he examined: the slippers, the candle, Zaremba's nightshirt and Gorgonowa's nightgown, his underwear, her brassiere, a piece of a match with blood on it, plaster scraped from the wall, the pillows, the comforter, the door and window frames. Then he lists which blood group was found on the individual objects.

Most important of all is the fur coat. Dr. Westfalewicz affirms what was leaked to the press a few weeks ago: spectroscopic and benzidine methods of testing found traces of type A blood on the lining. Westfalewicz's analyses incriminate Gorgonowa more than Staś's testimony because there is no way she could have gotten blood on herself other than during the murder. This dispels all doubts. For the moment.

Yet just after a short recess, disaster strikes. Judge Antoniewicz asks Dr. Piro to carefully examine the ice-axe retrieved from the pool and answer whether it could have been used to kill Zarembianka.

Dr. Karol Piro, who has just written in his autopsy report that it was probably the murder weapon, is now more cautious.

"It is possible and conceivable," he replies defensively. But when Axer presses him, he changes his opinion. He says it's unlikely Zarembianka was killed with an axe.

The courtroom murmurs in surprise and Prosecutor Laniewski's eyes go wide.

And that's only the beginning because a moment later, Dr. Piro says the murder was a lust killing committed by a man.

Before the stunned courtroom can recover its senses, an old man in horn-rimmed glasses speaks up. He is an expert chemist, Dr. Jan Opieński. He says it's possible that type A blood belonging to Lusia was found on Gorgonowa's fur coat—but it's impossible to state that with total certainty because the testing method used is antiquated and not particularly accurate.

Next to address the court is thirty-six-year-old Professor Józef Dadlez, an expert from the Lwów Institute of Forensic Medicine.

"Do you believe the deceased's hymen was broken by a woman?" Axer asks him.

"More likely a man," Dadlez replies uncertainly.

"Do the injuries match the defendant's fingers?" asks the defense counsel.

Dadlez and Piro approach the accused. She stands and reaches out her hands, which the experts examine carefully. They confer briefly.

Dadlez speaks up. He says the wound on the hymen was larger than the defendant's fingers.

Gorgonowa falls into spasms of weeping. Dadlez tries to rescue the situation, to soften what he's just said, so he states that Gorgonowa's slim fingers could still have broken Zarembianka's hymen. But this doesn't change anything. The expert witnesses' testimony leaves everyone's heads spinning. Now no one has any idea how this breathtaking trial will turn out.

The next day the newspapers report the sensational twist in Lwów: "The trial is beginning to grow obscure and convoluted in an incredible way, for the expert testimony, contrary to the expectations of the court and public opinion, did not shine the anticipated light on the case. Both the panel of judges and the jurors will be proceeding blindly as they consider this remarkable criminological mystery."

The expert witness testimonies are a blow to the prosecution. Instead of finally incriminating Gorgonowa, they give her compelling arguments for her defense and calls the entire indictment into question. According to the law, whatever is uncertain and unconfirmed always counts in favor of the defendant. Now two key pieces of evidence have fallen away: the fur coat and the murder weapon. Laniewski must feel the turning point. He must feel the scales tilting against him.

To prove Gorgonowa's innocence, Axer demands that the court carefully examine the records of the unsolved murder of twelve-year-old Józia Neuwerówna in Lwów. In the defense's view, the circumstances and injuries of both victims are remarkably similar, meaning both crimes were committed by the same unknown perpetrator.

And to undermine the credibility of key testimony by Staś Zaremba, Axer insists the boy undergo psychiatric assessment.

To prove it would be impossible to distinguish Gorgonowa's willow-green nightgown from her white one at night, he calls for the renowned painter Andrzej Pronaszko to testify.

Axer claims that only a professional criminal would defecate at the scene of the crime. (Inspector Piątkiewicz, author of a textbook for the State Police, is meant to confirm this.)

He shows that the servant Beckerówna is a frequent liar, so her testimony of what Gorgonowa allegedly said after Lusia's death— "God, what have I done?"—is unreliable. (Józef Jedwab, one of Beckerówna's recent employers, is meant to confirm this.)

"We must declare that total disorientation came over not only the gallery, but many jurors too," says *Ilustrowany Kurier Codzienny*, summing up Saturday's proceedings.

A MUDDLE

Lwów, Monday, May 2, 1932

"Public opinion in Lwów has divided into two fundamental camps: women and men," writes the Warsaw nationalist newspaper *Nowiny Codzienne*. "The female world is more energetic, being led mainly by Jewish women, who have packed the courtroom en masse, are living newspapers, and know everything 'for certain.' The male camp is calmer and relies not on moods, but facts."

Even the sections of Lwów's press that are critical of Gorgonowa are now changing tack, noting that not everything is as unambiguous as it had previously seemed. Tongues are wagging all over Lwów. Until Saturday the evidence against Gorgonowa was strong and incontrovertible, then turned completely worthless. It's hard to grasp. Lwów wants to find out more, so people stand out on Batory Street in front of the courthouse, which is closed on Sundays. Rumor has it Professor Antoni Westfalewicz got to the presiding judge after court adjourned and persuaded him that he'd been misunderstood. He asked the court for the chance to explain himself during Monday's proceedings.

Monday begins with Westfalewicz's clarifications.

He describes the complexities of blood testing performed by the Lattes method, which he used in his analyses. He says tests have been done this way for many years around the world and have served as the basis for criminal convictions. He knows there is a more modern and more precise method, but he assures the court that the results of his tests are entirely sufficient.

"The blood from the fur coat is type A and it is Zarembianka's blood," he says. "That is my most profound conviction."

The court does not share this optimism. The method Leone Lattes invented is imperfect because it gives inaccurate results for type O, which Gorgonowa has. So this evidence cannot be considered.

The judges decide to adjourn and commission another expert analysis from the State Institute of Hygiene in Warsaw. It is run by the world-famous serologist Professor Ludwik Hirszfeld, who created the blood typing system that is used to this day and who also discovered the laws governing blood type heritability. He is the greatest pre-war authority on this subject.

This is a great victory for the defense. Axer has managed to sow doubt in the minds of the jurors. The expert witnesses have been a tremendous help, particularly Professor Antoni Westfalewicz, who during his cross-examination undermined his own testing method, calling all of his findings into question. Today he's been trying to save face by explaining he was misunderstood.

But can he be trusted?

POSTHASTE!

Lwów, Saturday, May 14, 1932

On Wednesday, May 4, the Sate Institute of Hygiene in Warsaw received a package, tied up with string and sealed with stamps of the District Court in Lwów. Inside was the most important item of evidence—the brown fur coat—as well as candles, door handles, handkerchiefs, and pieces of the porch wall, doors, plaster, and windowpanes.

Enclosed in the package is a letter from Presiding Judge Antoniewicz. He writes that the matter is very urgent, that he has adjourned the trial until May 14 and that by then he must receive an expert opinion from Hirszfeld; if he doesn't have time, they will have to start the trial all over again.

"FOR THIS REASON THE TESTING MUST ABSOLUTELY BE CONDUCTED SUCH THAT BY THE MORNING OF MAY 13 AT THE LATEST THE MATERIAL EVIDENCE AS WELL AS THE RESULTS AND THE EXPERT ANALYSIS ARE AT THE COURTHOUSE IN LWÓW." Judge Antoniewicz types his most important request in capital letters.

"The tests will be finished by the required deadline," forty-eight-year-old Hirszfeld writes back.

This is now the focus of his attention. The newspapers write that the fate of the trial is in his hands, and he only has eight days for all the tests.

"At the time I was as popular as an opera diva," recalled Hirszfeld in his memoirs.

> I found this remarkably unpleasant. I stopped going near the telephone since newspaper offices were inundating me with questions; my secretary at the institute and my wife at home refused to give any kind of information. Yet once I was caught out. "Professor, we'd like to ask you for a photograph." "Unfortunately I must refuse, on principle I don't give publications my likeness because I find this form of popularity unpleasant." In response I heard: "We understand completely and we truly apologize." I said to my wife: "Finally, a sensitive reporter." My optimism turned out to be misplaced. The very next day my photograph appeared in the paper; God knows who gave it to them.

On the morning of May 12, Professor Hirszfeld sends a telegram to Lwów: "Expert report finished. I am dispatching it by express this evening."

"The expert analysis from Warsaw is simply sensational," writes *Nowiny Codzienne*. "All of Lwów has once again caught fever."

On the black market, tickets to the last day of the trial are already fetching the astronomical price of fifty złotys, and at lottery stands you can place bets: execution or acquittal.

"Unfortunately," recalled Hirszfeld, "people turned the judicial proceedings into something like a tournament, which was contrary to my will and intention."

"No other day of the trial was anticipated with such tension," writes Prosecutor Laniewski.

> Indeed, the time had come to read out the results of the chemical expert's analysis of the blood, to which

public opinion had attached great, maybe even exaggerated, importance. That day the prosecution and defense counsel were also to speak. Finally, to end that day, the verdict was to be reached, resolving this whole complicated criminal incident. Hence the crowd of people was larger than it had ever been thus far.

As early as six in the morning, small groups of people are hanging around on Batory Street, trying to scheme how to get inside the courthouse. But ticket inspection has been tightened up and the police presence has been fortified. Not even all the ticketholders are able to get into the courtroom.

After nine o'clock, amid great anticipation, Presiding Judge Antoniewicz reads out the serological test report. Over twenty typewritten pages, Professor Hirszfeld's team has delivered a hermetic, scientific disquisition on the chemistry of blood. It is convoluted and incomprehensible to the uninitiated. The most important part of it is a single sentence:

"Tests employing the most sensitive method of detecting element A on the lining of the defendant's fur coat—the presence of element A, originating in the blood, was not demonstrated."

Nor was it present on the handkerchief found in the cellar.

"My response, rejecting to some extent the findings of previous experts, literally shook the country," wrote Hirszfeld.

It is a massive blow for Laniewski.

"I have never before encountered such contradictions in the opinions of experts," the prosecutor protests to the court.

He tries to save face and rescue the indictment, explaining to the jurors that the scientific report is of little import for the case because the other evidence is overwhelming. At the same time he tries to convince the court to order another round of tests, this time from the medical school of the University of Lwów. The doctors there would be asked to compare the reports of all the experts and determine which ones contained errors and what, if any, joint conclusions could be drawn from them.

The court rejects his motion, closes the evidentiary phase of the trial, and adjourns for lunch—a sign that everything will be over today.

In photographs from the trial, Laniewski looks like a diligent student hunched over his notebook as he scribbles down the most important sections of testimony. The notes he's been keeping for a week are now meant to help him persuade the jurors.

"I realized that despite what I, at this point, considered a completely clear case, doubts could arise in the minds of the jurors," recalled Laniewski.

> I also understood how very much at this moment it depended on me for truth to triumph, and justice along with it.
> I stood, leaning on the frame of the door leading from the courtroom to the conference room. In the courtroom, jammed with people, there wasn't a peep. No one budged an inch.

Laniewski broke the silence with the prosecution's closing argument:

> When the scrolls of files lay on my desk, the rustling of which suggested to my lively imagination the wails of the murdered victim, I was overcome by one determination: to bind my hands, so they would not yearn to do something reckless, restrain my emotions so they could not lash out, and then I resolved to maintain a

sober eye, a calmness, to wrack my brain, sharpen my vision, to look truth in the face.

And he paints a picture of the defendant as the wickedest of the wicked: an unfeeling egotist aiming only to advance her own interest. Cold, ruthless, brimming with hate for everyone who stands in her way.

Prosecutor Laniewski has written down the most important quotes from the witness testimony. He juggles them to corroborate what a bad child-carer she was, how she saw Zaremba's children as a burden and source of unnecessary expenses. Everything negative that was said about her in the courtroom is now scrupulously recalled. Every sentence and every word.

He speaks warmly of Lusia—of how she suffered as a stranger took the place of her mother.

"I doubt whether Lusia at that age was capable of hate. But I know that Gorgonowa was. She began to speak of killing Lusia."

The prosecutor once again relies on his notes, evokes the facts and the witness testimonies. All this to persuade the jurors that conflict was mounting between Lusia and Rita. That Rita saw Lusia as the cause of her troubles. And that once she understood that because of Lusia, the door to the Zarembas' new apartment on Potocka Street would be closed to her, Rita decided to eliminate her rival.

In the prosecution's view, the motive for the killing was hatred and revenge for her broken fate. For Zaremba turning his back on her. Gorgonowa believed that once the daughter was eliminated everything would be as it was before, and she would move back in with Henryk.

After two hours of speaking, Laniewski asks for a brief recess.

A short while later, he strikes with full force. Now he focuses on the murder itself and the considerable—he says—evidence of guilt. He says most important of all is the testimony of young Staś Zaremba.

"When he stated that the mysterious figure in the foyer was Gorgonowa, he did not yet know she was suspected of the murder," the prosecutor reminds them.

Laniewski points out the other circumstantial evidence implicating the defendant. The footprints in the snow, the injured hand, the broken windowpane, the candle, the handkerchief, the willow-green nightgown, which was never found but still points to her guilt. And the bloodied fur coat, about which the experts delivered contradictory opinions.

He reminds them of the maid, Tobiaszówna, who testified under oath that when Gorgonowa learned the police had found footprints leading to her porch, she said: "Oh God, oh God, what have I done?"

Gorgonowa's fate is in the hands of the twelve jurors. They know the facts; now they must feel the emotions. Finally, Laniewski speaks only to them.

"In a few moments I am to conclude my remarks, and I am overcome with great trepidation: have I lived up to this great task? Have I been so clear that I have managed to persuade you gentlemen[1] of this truth, which is plain to see and in which I believe? So permit me to say another few final words. No longer as a prosecutor to a jury, but man to men, citizen to citizens, father to fathers. Believe me, gentlemen, I have not handled this case the way files are ordinarily read. I have lived and breathed this case. I have delved into its innermost recesses. It has shredded my nerves, disrupted the peace of my days and nights. I have followed the perpetrator step by step, wandered by the pool, walked around the hall, followed the perpetrator to the cellar, watched her hand as she killed, I have walked like a ghost, like a malicious spirit, driven by a great, absolute imperative, one purpose: justice must prevail!"

He pauses briefly.

"My whole being cries out to you: it was she who did it!" he thunders menacingly. "Everything around me, the trees in the forests of

---

1 There were no women on the jury.

Brzuchowice, the bricks of that unhappy villa, the walls of the court-room, the cobblestones cry out: 'She killed!' Heaven and earth cry out: 'She killed!'"

Another short pause. Then he continues, more gently:

"When you gentlemen retire to the conference room to issue your final judgment, crawling after you will be the ghost of a girl unde-servedly murdered. Do not turn your face from her, look upon her, though where bright eyes should be, only sockets turn to you, though her childish body be eaten away by the earth. Look at her still. She raises toward you the tibiae of her arms, points a fleshless finger at you and in a quiet voice from beyond the grave she whispers: 'It is she who killed me.'"

Laniewski would later write that by the time he finished his state-ment, it was dark outside the windows. The courtroom was deathly silent. No one moved an inch. There wasn't the slightest murmur.

"To me, that was a great moment in my life, when I had stopped speaking but the courtroom was still listening," he wrote. ("All the lucky ones who managed to make it into the courtroom are still in awe of the prosecution's fantastic closing statement, a speech of a kind rarely heard in a courtroom," writes *Gazeta Wieczorna* the next day.)

A half an hour later, Maurycy Axer makes his response. ("That wise, experienced defender knew well where the truth lay," noted La-niewski. "That made his duty all the harder.")

"When the public opinion of our city formed a united front against the defendant, when curses and insults came at her from all sides, when the crowd extended its fists over her head, mercilessly brandishing a noose, and for many of Lwów's citizens the person of the executioner became the symbol of law and justice, when every-one, far and near, turned away from the defendant, leaving her alone with her boundless misfortune, I stood beside her, so as with her and for her to fight for her honor, freedom, and life. I am no equal to the preceding speaker in my choice of words and arguments. I will not reach those heights of eloquence that his statement attained. I exceed him in only one thing: in the strength of my conviction that in this case, the champion of truth is not the prosecutor, but I myself. There is but one truth. Today it is with me and together with me it cries out, loud and clear, that Rita Gorgonowa is innocent! Yet I tremble for the fate of the defendant, I am overcome with doubts in human justice and with desperate anxiety in premonition of what will follow in this courtroom. For before me stands my opponent, a hundred times more powerful than I, whom I am not able to vanquish. A mighty and invincible enemy, who crushes everyone and everything under his weight. Blind to the glaring light of truth, deaf to the cry of the human soul, unmoved by the most straightforward arguments, cold, wicked, cruel public opinion, much more rightly called the voice of the street, has already delivered its verdict on Rita Gorgonowa, has long since slammed shut the lid of the coffin into which you, distinguished members of the jury, are supposed to place her today. But the voice of the street has never been the voice of God."

Axer must know he is on a hopeless mission. He has against him not only the prosecution, the journalists, and the gallery, which mutters all throughout his statement, but also thousands of those who have been waiting since dawn on Batory Street for the death sentence. They cannot imagine another verdict.

Axer attempts to thwart those expectations. He turns the tables. He makes Gorgonowa out to be a victim, recounting how difficult it was for her when her husband left her and her baby at the mercy of her in-laws, who treated her like an enemy. How she had to fight for survival in a foreign country.

He accuses the prosecutor of being unable to find Lusia's murderer—for, he assures the jury, it is not Rita Gorgonowa.

"A sexual murder has definitely taken place here," he explains. "The savagery of this act speaks against the defendant's guilt," he continues, paying no heed to the periodic groans in the courtroom. "The only perpetrator who could have done this was groundskeeper Kamiński. All the circumstances of the investigation point to him."

Before he moves on to his final attack, he dispenses with the unreliable testimony. He does not accuse the witnesses of lying. He speaks instead of ill will and submitting to collective psychosis.

He questions each piece of evidence:

"This is not proof, it is circumstantial evidence, and even this circumstantial evidence has been invalidated during the trial."

He reminds them that the foundation of the indictment was the blood analysis.

"Yet this foundation collapsed," he emphasizes.

He appeals to the jurors:

"Remember all those who have ended up on the scaffold because of the errors of courts. Don't allow the defendant's innocent, fifteen-year-old son [Erwinek] to spend his whole life bearing a mark of shame when his mother is sentenced to death."

Rita sobs for the whole of Axer's speech. Tears are still flowing from her blue eyes when Presiding Judge Antoniewicz encourages her to have the last word.

"Your honor!" she says, weeping. "I am just as much this criminal's victim as Lusia, may she rest in peace. Before God and man I declare that I am innocent."

The jury retires to deliberate while the gallery argues: guilty, not guilty, death, or acquittal?

Only Prosecutor Laniewski has no doubt: "The thing was totally comprehensible: As matters stand, the case could no longer rouse the slightest doubts in anyone with a head on his shoulders."

After nineteen minutes, the conference doors open behind the judges. The arguments die down. The twelve jurors cross the room in utter silence, sit down in the box, and only the jury foreman, Dr. Kazimierz Hofmokl, approaches the bench with a piece of paper in his hand.

"To the question of whether Emilia Margarita Gorgonowa is guilty of the murder of Elżbieta Zarembianka, the jury responds with nine votes 'yes,' and three votes 'no.'"

Guilty. Yet the courtroom is shocked the verdict is not unanimous and bursts out in anger.

Gorgonowa is also shaken, as if she didn't expect this. She slides down in her chair and hangs her head limply. She leans on the shoulder of the policeman sitting next to her, who whispers something to her.

"He spoke to her like a father cheering up an unhappy daughter," notes the writer Elga Kern, who is observing the trial.

"As the foreman of the jury read out the verdict, she took in everything that had happened. This woman, who had cried for almost the duration of the defense's closing argument, went completely calm after the verdict; and when the defense counsel, to raise her spirits, told her that not all was yet lost, she replied with only a melancholy nod of the head," writes Kern.

After the jury's verdict, the court's sentence is obvious, yet the court is obliged to pronounce it. Now the judges need only apply the appropriate section of the Penal Code. The Austrian Penal Code provides only one punishment for murder—execution by hanging. (A mere few months later, a new, more liberal code will come into force, which will allow the courts to choose various levels of sentencing.)

When Rita Gorgonowa is condemned to death, she is thirty-one years old, she has no family, friends, acquaintances, no one who could help her. And she is in the fifth month of a pregnancy with the child of the man whose daughter she is accused of killing.

When around 11 P.M. the prison van takes Rita to Brygidki Prison, a carnival is still taking place outside the District Court on Batory Street. Thousands of Lwów's citizens have come to congratulate one another on the sentence that has just been handed down. Now they will wait for the punishment to be carried out. In pre-war Poland, that usually meant a few weeks to a few months.

RITA'S DEFENSIVE FRONT

Warsaw, Sunday, June 19, 1932

She is forty-six and has dark hair, light-colored eyes, and a narrow mouth. That's how she looks in a photo taken in 1931 in the Polskie Radio studio in Lwów, where she was delivering a talk on the need for cultural rapprochement between Germans and Poles.

At the trial she sits somewhere near Gorgonowa and watches her closely, carefully describing her behavior, gestures, facial expressions. She is in a picture taken by a photographer for *Ilustrowany Kurier Codzienny* assigned to the trial in Lwów, there among the exuberant men and women who every day come to court as if it were the movies.

She is German. Her name is Elga Kern. The Polish press calls her a "brilliant woman of letters."

And she's remarkably brave. In Germany, where more and more men are marching under black banners, she—a Jew—is still fighting for women's rights.

In the late twenties and early thirties she takes two long trips to Poland, visiting cities like Gdynia, Wilno, Łódź, and Lwów. The fruit of her fascination with Poland is a book published in Zürich in 1931: *Vom alten und neuen Polen* ("From Old and New Poland"). In it, interwar Poland appears as an oasis of happy and hard-working people, a country of great culture, great history, and great prospects. In Germany, where Adolf Hitler is making swift strides toward power, Elga Kern's publication goes almost unnoticed. But in Poland she is very popular.

"The book is written with an enthusiasm that shuns the tasteless exaggerations of propaganda publications. Elga Kern could not give us a better recommendation," writes Poland's most important prewar cultural periodical, *Wiadomości Literackie*, about her book.

Years later, it's in *Wiadomości* that Kern places one of her most famous pieces, titled "The Truth About the Gorgonowa Trial." In it, she questions the accuracy of the trial and the reliability of the witnesses and evidence.

Kern arrives in Lwów from Mannheim, near the French border, where she has lived for years. The press are not the only ones to notice her appearance at the trial; she even catches Prosecutor Laniewski's eye: "She hangs around Lwów like some purported 'foreign author,' who has simply flung passionate invective and insults at me," he writes, "as if the Gorgonowa trial were my personal affair, and as if I could have any other interest in all of this than the interest of justice, which I represent."

"I have come not to defend Rita Gorgonowa, but to defend the cause of Rita Gorgonowa," she explains to Polish journalists. "I have spoken out against this great miscarriage of justice. I take the unaltered position that psychologically it is an impossible thing that a woman could be accused of such a crime."

"Who in your opinion could have committed the crime, if you rule out Rita Gorgonowa?"

"I do not in the least rule out an outside person," she replies. "To me, Gorgonowa would be suspected right alongside the other members of the household."

"But Staś saw her in the foyer."

"Every psychologist knows that a boy at the age of maturation falls under the influence of the moon," replies Kern assuredly, "and on the night of the murder the moon was full. It's possible that Staś, under the moon's influence, imagined many things he didn't see."[2]

She is the first to publicly defend Rita Gorgonowa. She stands firmly by her, supports her, agitates on her behalf, and boldly postulates that Staś Zaremba accused Gorgonowa under the influence of lunar rays.[3]

The fact that she speaks Polish poorly and writes her articles only in German makes no difference. She's a much higher profile figure than the dozens of journalists dependably reporting the trial every day. Her voice carries more weight because it can be heard around Europe as well.

Her essay, or rather her feminist manifesto in defense of Rita Gorgonowa, is published in *Wiadomości Literackie*, a weekly paper headquartered at 8 Złota Street in Warsaw, run by a group of left-leaning authors.

Elga Kern attacks everyone who had a hand in condemning Gorgonowa: the police, the prosecutor's office, the court, and even Zaremba who, she writes, incriminated his partner based on unclear circumstantial evidence.

She points out mistakes. The police wanted to catch the criminal so quickly that they didn't examine all the witnesses and all the traces of the crime. The material evidence is "tragicomically worthless"—everything is based on hypotheses, on circumstantial evidence, and on motive. And nothing has been proven.

---

2 "Nie bronię Rity Gorgon, lecz bronię sprawy Rity Gorgon. Sensacyjny wywiad »Expressu« z p. Elgą Kern" [I Do Not Defend Rita Gorgon, but I Defend the Cause of Rita Gorgon: Sensational *Express* Interview with Mrs. Elga Kern], *Express Wieczorny Ilustrowany*, March 26, 1933.

3 "Coraz więcej głosów za uniewinnieniem Gorgonowej" [More and More Voices in Favor of Acquitting Gorgonowa], *Nowiny Codzienne*, March 25, 1933.

She doesn't like that the jury of twelve is made up of only re-tired military officers and policemen, and does not include a single woman.

"From the very start everything was immediately prejudiced toward Gorgonowa's guilt, and the police investigation, the clever gutter-press and so-called public opinion all walk hand-in-hand in stunning unity. Everything was explained to the detriment of this woman and each detail was turned against her, while everything that might have spoken to her benefit was muffled and passed over in silence by the press. So the life of a mother of two children, with a third on the way, was turned into the helpless plaything of the masses lusting for sensation," she writes in her article.

> Everyone who has been to Lwów even in passing must be struck and shaken to the core that here, of all places, where there are so many churches and so many servants of God, a person should be treated like a stray dog. How warmly we should wish that the spirit that people claim to be the premise of a trial would also take some interest in Gorgonowa's.
>
> We witnessed day after day on the streets of Lwów revolting pamphlets against the defendant being sold and loudly touted left and right, and at no point could anyone calm, removed from this dreadful underhandedness and resistant to grubby suggestions, speak up to express his justified doubts and reservations.

Elga Kern rigorously interrogates each piece of circumstantial and material evidence. She calls into doubt the course of events, the mo-tive for the crime, the murder weapon, and whether Gorgonowa was capable of committing murder at all.

117

Our point is not whether Gorgonowa is guilty or innocent, but only that, if she is guilty, she ought to have been proven so, not by sticking her with some motive that may or may not exist, but by confirmed facts.

Since in this trial all the circumstantial evidence has turned out to be shaky, the question arises: how could the jury have scrounged up its certainty that the defendant was guilty?

Lastly, Kern writes that the judicial authorities refused her permission to visit the pregnant Gorgonowa.

"I thought it was my humane, womanly duty to go to her and say that in her doubly burdened position she was not left completely on her own."

Elga Kern's article sets off a firestorm.

In the nationalist daily *ABC*, the well-known commentator Irena Pannenkowa pushes back against her.

"The way she speaks about the prosecutor, an official of the Polish State, doesn't seem proper, even if she weren't a foreigner. One gets the impression that Mrs. Kern held it against the prosecutor for accusing and not defending. But the function of a prosecutor is to accuse. Such a duty may seem unkind, yet nonetheless, duty it is."

Gazeta Wieczorna: "Mrs. Elga Kern has a partisan view of the case. She ferrets out all the mistakes of the judicial proceedings and the investigation, while discreetly casting a blind eye on a string of hard facts to which she either does not know how to respond, or does not care to."

The main charge against Kern is camouflaged, but we can read it between the lines of these commentators: a German woman shouldn't stick her nose in, shouldn't stir things up. Let her mind her own German business.

Kern responds to this unspoken accusation in *Wiadomości Literackie*:

> I have done my utmost to demonstrate that issues exist outside the realm of national sentiment that can drive a writer to intervene out of a sense of responsibility for her era and the future. If the Gorgonowa case were a matter of a political trial, I would never get involved, either in a foreign country or in my own homeland. As a German I could intervene in a political trial abroad only under strictly defined circumstances.
>
> When it comes to the Gorgonowa trial, the issue appears completely different. This is a humanitarian issue that concerns me as a European writer, concerns me fundamentally, and compels me to act. In any event, we cannot demand of anyone that they remain silent about a death sentence that goes against their deepest convictions.
>
> What, therefore, have I undertaken since the death sentence in Gorgonowa's trial in Lwów? I had a conversation in Warsaw with a certain writer whom I greatly respect and who is valued by all of Poland. We invited a certain lawyer into our conference. After mature, collective consideration, I expressed my readiness to formulate for these two gentlemen a substantive report from the trial. It was later made public in *Wiadomości Literackie*. As for me—I emphasize strongly—I would have preferred a hundred times over for such a report to have been made public at that time by a Polish writer.
>
> To be sure, terrible things are happening all over the world, no one feels that more painfully at this mo-

ment than I, and yet even today, if I found myself at the beginning of the trial, I would not be able to proceed other than as I have.

Must a country's standing really suffer because a woman stood alongside one of her sisters, because a German writer in Poland offered her knowledge and sense of responsibility in the service of humanitarianism, as she had already done many times in other circumstances and as she will do again in the future?

A few days ago a fifteen-year-old boy, the son of Rita Gorgonowa, placed his hand in mine and said, "Please don't abandon my mother. My mommy didn't do this. I'm sure she didn't."

Is that not enough to awaken a sense of obligation? Was I to stop and wonder whether I am Polish or German?

This is not about Rita Gorgonowa, this is not about that boy, Erwin Gorgon, this is about a mother and son, about the nonexistent proof that a mother of three children is guilty.[4]

The readers of *Wiadomości Literackie* appreciate the German woman's bravery. They send her letters of support via the editorial office. A pro-Gorgonowa movement forms around the newspaper, and grows stronger, louder, and more convincing with every day.

The writer Stanisława Przybyszewska, living in Danzig and known for her play *The Danton Case*, writes to Kern in German, in blue ink on pages torn out of a notebook:

"I do not wish to flatter you, but your standing up for Gorgonowa in Lwów itself, and with your nationality besides . . . In your shoes I

---

4 "Wiele hałasu, a mało prawdy [Much Noise, but Little Truth]," letter from Elga Kern to the editors, *Wiadomości Literackie*, April 23, 1933.

would not have been brave enough. Why, for many months you have been risking your life."

This is a letter of gratitude for having the courage to declare her own views, for her determination and the strength of her argument. Kern can have no doubt that Przybyszewska also firmly believes Rita is the victim of a miscarriage of justice compelled by a hysterical mob.

Impoverished, sick, and starving, Przybyszewska lives in a barrack on Am Weißen Turm, where her only daily entertainment is reading the newspapers. The Gorgonowa case catches her serious interest only in late April 1932, shortly before the verdict is announced.

Przybyszewska recalled in her writings: "Only a week later did I see with cold dread that Mrs. Gorgonowa is no harpy, but first and foremost an ordinary person: that is, morally and mentally strong, performing well her life's maternal calling. At the same time I grasped that a terrible error not only might have, but by the law of human nature, must have befallen her: and this was due to the awful mediocrity of the people on whom responsibility had fallen."

Based on her own analysis of what she read in the news, and without leaving Danzig, she becomes firmly convinced that Gorgonowa is innocent. In the fate of this hounded, homeless, ostracized foreigner left at the mercy of local chauvinism, Przybyszewska recognizes her own story as an ethnic Polish citizen of the Free City of Danzig on the eve of the victory of Nazism. Gorgonowa's story moves her so much that in February 1933 she starts work on an outline of a drama about the case. *Drunken Themis* is to be a revolutionary play, attacking from the stage the soulless Lwów court and the prosecutor's office that were sending an innocent woman to death. The play is never finished.

But the letter in defense of Gorgonowa that Przybyszewska sends to the offices of *Wiadomości Literackie* is published in March 1933 on the front page.

The editors tout the article by Przybyszewska ("daughter of that marvelous writer Stanisław Przybyszewski") as a valuable complement to Elga Kern's memorable piece. Przybyszewska's letter is even more combative, but not very concrete. It is essentially an appeal to society to repair the harm the court has done to a poor woman. As she analyzes the specific evidence of guilt, Przybyszewska reaches completely different conclusions than the police, the prosecutor, the court, and the jurors. To her, all the evidence seems to speak for the defendant's innocence rather than her guilt.

"How can Mrs. Gorgonowa's case have gone to trial, how can she have been sentenced in the first place?" she writes, amazed, and then answers her own question:

> Unfortunately, it had to happen: contrary to reason, contrary to justice, but in accordance with the laws of human nature. The sudden sensation of the crime, notorious nationwide, proved too strong a temptation for Lwów's authorities. The mob, swollen with outrage, demanded a criminal: for the local police, not catching one would have been a failure. Meanwhile Mrs. Gorgonowa was at hand; what's more, as a woman, a foreigner, and above all as an unwedded partner, she was an exceptionally desirable target both for a prosecutor wishing to make a name for himself and for the mob, greedy for sensation.
>
> Therefore everyone—the court and the police for professional reasons, the mob for psychological ones—everyone desired for her to be the culprit. [...]
>
> Lwów found itself, before and during the trial, in a psychopathic state. This epidemic vortex of public opinion stripped us all, fortunately temporarily, of our

sanity, and so therefore of our responsibility when it came to Mrs. Gorgonowa. [...]

The unsubstantiated and vehement assuredness of Mrs. Gorgonowa's guilt was a natural, unavoidable result of this mental epidemic. Nearly all of us fell victim to it for a certain time: but the healthier we are mentally, the sooner reason will reassert authority within us. Then each of us must admit that an awful error has taken place.

At this very moment [...] there is an opportunity to repair this horrible error; an opportunity to give a thoroughly normal woman with an outstandingly maternal nature, who has undeservingly gone through hell, her life back. Finally, a wonderful opportunity to clear the name of the judiciary.

Does [the court] wish to, is it capable of seizing that chance?[5]

---

5 Stanisława Przybyszewska, "Rita Gorgon, ofiara zastępcza [Rita Gorgonowa, Scape-goat]," *Wiadomości Literackie*, March 12, 1933.

THE APPEAL

Warsaw, Thursday, July 21, 1932

Maurycy Axer is preparing for the appeal proceedings in apartment 317 at the Hotel Europejski on Warsaw's Krakowskie Przedmieście Street.

He must feel the gathering strength of those now convinced his client is innocent and was the victim of police incompetence and mutually contradictory expert scientists; that her guilt was determined not by the evidence, but by her sex, her foreign origin, and the hostile Lwów masses.

The doubtful have been growing in number ever since Axer's daring closing statement in mid-May. This change of mood is now reflected in the tone of the newspaper coverage of Gorgonowa's appeal.

The most popular publications now write about the doubts the Supreme Court must consider and which Axer has raised in filing his appeal. He accuses the Lwów court of committing an unforgivable error: omitting incredibly important evidence that he submitted for the defense. He lists ten errors, from declining to investigate a murder case in Lewandówka district, to rejecting requests for Staś and Rita to be psychiatrically assessed, to not calling as a witness the artist Zbigniew Pronaszko—who claims that at night, by candlelight, it is impossible to distinguish willow-green from white.

Axer is no longer alone. He will be assisted at the appeal hearing by a celebrity of the Warsaw Bar, forty-six-year-old Mieczysław Ettinger.

The newspapers mainly predict that the Supreme Court will overturn the conviction and Gorgonowa will get another trial.

"It's become obvious to everyone who has not yet completely lost faith in jurisprudential justice that the Supreme Court will strike down the conviction," writes Elga Kern in her notes. At the appeal hearing she sits in the first row.

Overseeing the hearing is Presiding Justice Witold de Michelis. Joining him on the panel are Justices Janusz Jamontt and Stanisław Wyrobek. The hearing begins at ten o'clock, but the climax will come several hours later, after a recess for lunch, when the defense takes the floor.

Everyone is waiting for Axer's statement.

"May it please the court," he begins solemnly, then reminds them that the Lwów trial took place in a haze of toxic sensation, and the masses had rendered their verdict on Gorgonowa from the very beginning.

"She was condemned before she could say a single word in her defense, she had been judged and found guilty," he says. "A jury is the voice of the people, and the voice of the people is often the voice of the street. And the street was convinced from day one that Gorgonowa committed the murder."

Axer does not attack. Axer requests. Axer explains.

"I do not complain of an improper verdict, but of the harm done in the proceedings well before the verdict. Since the trial took place in a rotten, stifling atmosphere, poisoned by the venom of hatred toward the defendant, I think the duty of the Supreme Court is to come to the rescue of the accused to counterbalance this tendency. During the evidentiary stage, all the defense's applications were rejected, and I was threatened with being removed as her defense counsel," he explains.

He assails the witness testimony, the material evidence, and the expert opinions.

Elga Kern writes: "Both defense statements formed a perfectly constructed whole and were fantastic trump cards in the battle not only for one threatened human life, but for justice per se. For we cannot weigh this whole case merely as the fate of a certain individual; on the contrary, here human rights as a whole are under threat."

The court must have an issue with the verdict because the justices' deliberations last over two hours. Only at around midnight does the Supreme Court speak. It overturns Gorgonowa's death sentence and sends the case for reconsideration to the District Criminal Court in Kraków.

According to reporters for *Ilustrowany Kurier Codzienny*, the crowd in front of the Krasiński Palace, where the court sits, receives the news of Gorgonowa's new trial with enthusiasm.

"Which guarantees the new trial will take place in a calm and composed atmosphere," writes *Ilustrowany Kurier Codzienny*.

Elga Kern in her commentary in *Wiadomości Literackie* cannot overpraise the wisdom of Presiding Justice de Michelis.

"He based his judgment in this case not only on his legal expertise, but also on his own human emotions," she writes.

"He could have set limits, prohibited references to the poisonous atmosphere of the Lwów trial that translated into the verdict, but he did not. This allowed him to become truly the highest representative of state justice," she writes, seeing the chance of final victory in Kraków. "The historical setting and whole psychological atmosphere of the city, which provides it a certain distance from the day's sensation, provides the highest guarantee of a peaceful trial, free of influence."[6]

---

6 Elga Kern, "Unieważnienie wyroku w sprawie Gorgonowej [Overturning the Sentence in the Gorgonowa Case]," *Wiadomości Literackie*, August 14, 1933.

WE'RE GOING TO HAVE A BABY

After arriving in Brzuchowice in 1924, Rita writes once again to America:

Dear Erwin, from the moment that I learned that you are alive and healthy, I have been walking around with my head spinning. I can't find a place for myself and I feel an unhappiness that will torment me endlessly for the rest of my life. I've written to you so many times and inquired with the Polish consulate. There they didn't know anything about you either, and letters addressed to you kept coming back "unknown."

Three years have passed this way. All that time I didn't know what to think of you, what to do with myself.

Because if I'd known that you were alive and thinking of me, I wouldn't have taken a step that I will never cease to regret for the rest of my days. I don't know, maybe you despise me, or condemn me with all your soul? I had no other way out. I had to do what I did, or else go onto the street, become like thousands of other unfortunates. It was hard for me to live without any help or anyone who might offer me selfless aid.

After my wandering I found a job in the home of my current husband, and seven months later I agreed to become his wife. He paid no heed to the gossip or anonymous letters with which he was bombarded. I could see that he genuinely loved me.

My body may now belong to another, yet you are too deeply rooted in my heart to tear out. In this world wicked people have cut us off from one another and destroyed our life, our happiness. Erwin, since I am now another man's wife, I can admit the truth to you. No human being will now fill the void in my life. To you first I gave my love, heart, and soul.

I swear to you on the head of our only son, that sole remnant of our love, that I never betrayed you in the full sense of that word until I already belonged to another.

"One day she told me, her voice full of emotion, that we were going to have a baby," writes Zaremba. "I felt joy and unease at the same time. [. . .] This baby would have to strengthen the bonds between me and Gorgonowa, and at the same time reveal her to a world that in truth does not tolerate such relationships, [. . .] but instead cruelly, sanctimoniously mocks when illegal love bears fruit. [. . .] This baby strengthened her connection to Brzuchowice more than that first visit to me in Lwów had."

"Romusia was born on April 14, 1928. The child could not be given the last name Zaremba," recalls Henryk in his book. "But though she was illegitimate, I did not view her as an intruder. Instead she was a ray of happiness in my home, accepted as a blessing from God."

He stood over her cradle in awe, Staś gazed delightedly into her blue eyes, while Lusia positively adored mothering her.

Zaremba:

> Only Rita was impatient toward her own child. The baby would cry and she'd give the tiny thing a smack.
> "In God's name, woman, what are you doing?"
> "I can't stand it when the brat cries."

Before Romusia was born, the relationship between Gorgonowa and Lusia had begun to sour. As Lusia grew older, things got worse until they entered a state of open warfare.

> A war between Gorgonowa and Lusia began in my home. A strange war, because one side continually attacked, while the other desperately and pitifully defended her position. She made no sorties, but rather retreated proudly and scornfully, saying with her eyes more than her words that she did not feel defeated.
>
> In every argument when Gorgonowa's voice dominated, when I held my tongue under a hail of shouts and affronts, my daughter's eyes would look at me pathetically, saying clearly: "Daddy, why is she hurting you like this? What does she want, this woman who is a stranger here?"
>
> She was embarrassed by my unmanliness, my docility, my capitulation.
>
> The gulf between us grew. After the storms of spring and the heat of summer came the frost of winter. I didn't throw her out then—she was Romusia's mother.

She would take our carriage back and forth to Lwów on her own, and we at home would be glad she was gone.

By the fall of 1931, Rita can sense it's all coming to an end. Zaremba isn't speaking to her. He avoids her. He stops giving her the money for household upkeep.

"Dear Henio," she writes to him in late 1931, with a trembling hand on letter paper:

> I am writing to you because I have no other way to get you to hear me out.
>
> I can't believe you have such disgusting plans for me. And your only goal is to get rid of me.
>
> So why won't you come to Brzuchowice and tell me everything I'm supposed to do and how? [...]
>
> You don't love me—that I now know. [...] Because a person who loves would never do what you have done to me, Henio. [...]
>
> Today you wish for my doom and destruction.
>
> [...]
>
> Why are you using poverty and unkindness to force me out of your home? A person with human emotions would not even drive animals out of their den in wintertime like this. But you wish to drive me out. [...]
>
> After devouring my loveliest youth you are tossing me away like junk you now find spoiled and useless.
>
> Man, have you quite lost your honor already? If you have no obligation toward me, have mercy on your poor child, who has barely begun to live and whose poor, sad eyes fill with tears out of love for you.

And when she hears any movement, she dashes off: "Maybe my dear daddy has come?" And she constantly pesters me with questions: "Why doesn't Daddy come to see his little Romusia?"

What can I tell her?

Why did you bring a child into the world if now you're capable of abandoning her?

And if you think that I will leave this child to you, then how wrong you are. This child is all my treasure and my happiness. So you, you heartless man, want to take away the only joy in my sad life?

If I leave, it will be with the child. I will wander for as long as I have strength. God will not abandon me. Maybe even my mother won't have a heart of stone like you do and will take me and my poor orphan in. And I will work, day and night, so her orphanhood won't be a burden and won't poison her earliest youth and childhood years. [. . .] My only hope and only happiness is my child, whom I want to live and die for. I will do my best to give her everything we both owe her. And you, Henio, I forgive for all the hurt and my tears. May God forgive you.

In an article, Elga Kern describes their later fate:

Gorgonowa became a prisoner spied on at every step by the servants and a girl who had only just ceased to be a child, while the master of the house didn't lift a finger to help her. It goes without saying that in such an atmosphere Rita must on several occasions have lost her composure. Despite this, she never once hit the children who had been given into her care.

One way or the other, by December the situation for the entire household had become simply unbearable, wherefore it was decided to separate, meaning that starting on January 1, Gorgonowa was to remain at the villa in Brzuchowice while Zaremba and the two older children were to move to Lwów. Resistances arose regarding little Roma, whom it seemed everyone loved equally. Both her mother—who had the inalienable right to her baby—and Lusia Zarembianka demanded the child for themselves. Gorgonowa, who for so long had been separated from her son—at this time aged fourteen but inaccessible to her, since her in-laws did not permit mother and son to meet—was not willing under any circumstances to agree to part from her daughter. In one letter, Gorgonowa writes that she snuck like a thief up to her in-laws' house in hopes of laying eyes on her son and was driven away like a thief by her in-laws. The significance to her of separating from her daughter can only be understood by those who know that people who grew up in difficult emotional circumstances nevertheless maintain a great sensitivity of soul, though on the outside they may display a certain harshness.

ON THE ROAD WITH KROPELKA

Lwów to Kraków, Saturday, November 26, 1932

Everything takes place under the greatest secrecy: the prison van's nighttime departure from Brygidki on Kazimierzowska Street, its arrival at the main train station in Lwów, and the fact that it is carrying Margarita Gorgonowa and Kropelka, or "droplet." That's what the journalists call her daughter Krystyna Ewa, born two months ago in the prison in Lwów. So far no picture of the girl has appeared in any newspaper.

The local train to Kraków leaves the main station at five minutes after midnight. A prison guard and two intelligence officers deliver Gorgonowa to the train car. A police escort leads her to a reserved compartment, so as not to cause a sensation. But it's too late for that, since she's already been recognized at the station in Lwów. Word goes from car to car that Gorgonowa is on board.

As soon as the train sets off, people get out of their seats and check through the compartments.

Nowy Dziennik writes: "None of the efforts of the escort, which was doing its best to shield the woman from prying eyes, were of any use. Despite covering the windows with coats, travelers made every effort to peek into the compartment, at least for a moment."

The railroad workers telegraph to one another about the notorious woman on the local train from Lwów. News of her arrival at each station mobilizes gawkers in the middle of the night in Przemyśl, Rzeszów, Tarnów.

Rail workers who've been let in on the secret come out on the platforms with their families and friends.

Nowy Dziennik: "News of the lady passenger [...] kept stirring up an enormous commotion in railroad circles. At every station, crowds of railroad officials came out, peeking curiously into the windows of the train."

In Kraków, there is already a crowd of photo reporters waiting for her at suburban Płaszów station. It's the same at the next stop—the main station—where the train arrives at 8:5o A.M.

Only once all the passengers have disembarked does the escort lead the prisoner off the train.

Dressed in a black coat, a veil over her face, with her baby in her arms. The journalists describe Gorgonowa as showing no signs of her protracted stay in prison.

The policemen lead her to the railroad police station, where in a moment a taxi pulls up. They and Gorgonowa ride to Senacka Street, to the former convent of the Discalced Carmelites that now holds St. Michael's Prison. She is placed in a two-person cell on the second floor.

"Anyone going about his business who finds his way to Poselska Street, which runs uphill from Planty Park toward Kraków city center, must pass a large, gray edifice forming the corner of Poselska and Senacka. Within a few steps of Poselska Street, big-city life is in full swing, trolleys and cars race along, the clamor of the city reverberates, but Poselska Street is steeped in silence."[7]

Here Gorgonowa will wait more than three months for her first trial in a Kraków court.

"Today, the heart of the judiciary no longer holds the vengeful emotions of an affronted society: public opinion no longer demands

---

7 "Proces Gorgonowej" [The Gorgonowa Trial], *Tajny Detektyw*, March 12, 1933.

blood for blood. Polish penal law seeks to punish the criminal more severely inasmuch as the findings of the trial show him to be a greater danger in the future."[8]

Gorgonowa is to be found innocent or guilty by twelve jurors, who will be directed only by their own consciences. A panel of judges will determine the sentence.

This is how *Tajny Detektyw* announces the trial of the decade: "'Whoever kills a human being shall be subject to the penalty of imprisonment for a minimum term of five years, or for life, or of execution,' reads article 225 of the Polish Penal Code. Today, death is no longer the sole and inevitable punishment for murder."[9]

8 Ibid.
9 Ibid.

A RE-RUN OF JUSTICE

Kraków, Tuesday, March 7, 1933

The streets leading to the medieval building of the District Court on Senacka Street have been closed by the police. Mounted officers are patrolling the area. The trial is taking place in a large courtroom on the second floor.

At around 9 A.M., a constable leads Gorgonowa through the small door that separates St. Michael's Prison from the courthouse.

She has three lawyers defending her: Maurycy Axer, a familiar face from Lwów, as well as Mieczysław Ettinger from Warsaw, and Józef Woźniakowski from Kraków. Representing the prosecution is Bohdan Szypuła.

Presiding over the trial is Alfred Jendl, accompanied by two judges of the criminal court—Leonard Solecki and Jan Ostręga.

Weighing Gorgonowa's guilt are twelve jurors, once again all men: two brewery managers (Perans and Krowicki), two landowners (Ponióski and Kawalec), two retired military officers (Captain Karwat and Lieutenant Lubowiecki), an industrialist (Otorowski), a merchant (Bielawski) and four retirees: a former school principal (May), a former school inspector (Karaszkiewicz), a former treasury official (Dębicki), and a former county executive (Kępiński).

One thing is certain: the inevitable death penalty that was Gorgonowa's sentence in Lwów might not be handed down now. The new Penal Code leaves the ultimate choice to the court: it will decide, death or prison.

I watch this trial through the eyes of Irena Krzywicka, a thirty-four-year-old feminist, vanquisher of narrow-mindedness and petty bourgeois mentalities, writer and commentator for *Wiadomości Literackie*. She doesn't even try to seem objective. She has come from Warsaw to Kraków to defend Gorgonowa, who, she writes, was hounded by journalists and condemned by the pious, bigoted ladies of Lwów.

She describes the Kraków trial in 1933 in a series of three articles in *Wiadomości Literackie*.[10]

She writes:

> I am not a lawyer, and the advantage of these studies may solely be the very fact that they were not written by a lawyer, but by someone from the crowd, someone who has come off the street and seen from another angle. The daily press grasps the storyline of the trials, let a writer indulge in analysis.
>
> Twelve jurors, three judges, two prosecutors, three defense lawyers, experts, clerks, stenographers. Among them a woman, petrified and motionless, her face drained of blood, sometimes nervously stroking two fingers on her palm. For now I will not address whether Gorgonowa is guilty or innocent, but I must say that this mass of gloating men, in a giant circle surrounding this broken woman, is an immeasurably sorry sight, visually almost unbearable. We've grown used to seeing women everywhere. The lack of them

---

10 "Great Judicial Maneuvers" (in issue no. 23), "A Vision and Ghosts" (no. 24) and "A History of Sins ... Hers and Others"" (no. 25).

here, when the fate of a woman is at stake, is wrong, is practically offensive.

Yes. There are also women in the gallery. Tousle-haired, gray-headed Furies, mawkish little Furies. Permed, diamond-studded, eager for human flesh— giant Furies. Most of them swoon with regret that this time they won't get to see someone broken on the wheel or impaled on a stake.

Gorgonowa behaves "badly." Gloomy, stony-faced, her fur coat pulled up under her chin, often hunched over. No smiles or coyness or showing her neckline. When I heard people familiar with trials by jury speaking begrudgingly about this behavior, I shook with terror. One well-known lawyer told me about defending a woman who'd killed her husband. "The prospects of conviction were very bad, but she was a smart woman. Whenever she stood up, whenever she turned around, all the jurors craned their necks. They acquitted her."

But Gorgonowa can't even be persuaded to take off her fur coat.

The hours slowly crawl by. Faces sagging with expectation and fatigue, punctured again and again by nervous yawns. The hard benches, made of wooden planks, dig into the body.

Eyes staring blankly at the yellowish squares of windows with a view of a wall, from which they suck the lazy reflection of sunlight. Little shivers of cold, anxiety and weariness. On the ceiling, plump Themis clutches a scale.

I was seeing a trial by jury for the first time in my life and I had the full impression that you'd have just as much luck flipping a coin: heads or tails. The anxiety of what will tip the scales at the last moment, whether sentimental instinct or some secondary influence, maybe from one colleague with a stronger sense of individuality, or from the foreman?

Supporters of trial by jury claim that, unlike routine and class-influenced trial by government officials, a jury is the voice of the people. Meanwhile it's hard to imagine a more class-influenced jury than this one in Kraków, the majority of whom are retired or middle-aged gentlemen with government positions.

A people's court that includes not one proletarian, not one woman, no one young?

After all, the Gorgonowa trial relates to many complex questions demanding significant preparation. This chaos of details is difficult to master.

How can we demand that people unfamiliar with the law, with scientific issues, preoccupied with their own business, work out all the complexities of the trial here? This is a total lack of responsibility for the verdict, it's anonymity of action and handing justice over to reflex, to instinct, to chance impulse.

THROUGH KRZYWICKA'S EYES

Brzuchowice, Saturday, March 18 – Sunday, March 19, 1933

Krzywicka comes to Brzuchowice, where the court is conducting a site visit. We look at Zaremba's luxury villa through the eyes not of a provincial, but of a sophisticated woman from Warsaw.

The car taking me stopped in front of a "well-to-do" entrance gate. The base and the rails are almost as lavish as in a suburban housing development. An imitation of a noble manor house on half a morga of land. In a little garden, a clump of dreadful plaster statues, lions, grottos, temples, unbelievably packed together. Everything falling apart, crumbling.

Sodden walkways, the first mischievous little blades of grass sticking to your shoes, the defiant whiff of life floating on the breeze, the impudently bare sun. So jolly! Mr. Zaremba feels that jollity as he and Staś giggle in his family circle.

In an empty room, a woman sits hunched in a chair. She has a fever. Two policemen are guarding her— she's harmless. I can see her through the window—a black ghost divided by the windowpane from the white ghosts of the garden.

A dense crowd of indifferent and inquisitive people teems around the walkways. They are plastered to the windows, pressed up against the doors.

The white balustrade running in a square is the pool in which the ice-axe was found. (The pool looks more like a family tomb—a deep well with steps leading down into it). Further in, a high wall, impassable, attentively guarding the small amount of water, reeking with icy subterranean breath. This type of garden decorations could only be born of the imagination of a construction businessman who thought of himself as an "artist," drunk on provincial dreams of importance.

This tomb, these statues, this morbid decoration! Is it a coincidence that this is the place where criminality made itself at home?

We enter the villa. Here the image changes. Homey, "gemütlich," "uyutno," "sweet," and absurd, like most bourgeois interiors. The young girl's room with no door, forming an alcove in the foyer. Is that so that the little miss would live practically outside?

The dining room windows look out onto the kitchen. In the tiny bedroom of the lady of the house there are four doors. Everything is perfectly cramped, uncomfortable, and pointless.

In this uncomfortable and falsely homey interior, only one element is surprising: that it was possible to commit a crime here at all. The dining room where Staś slept, the foyer, and Lusia's alcove are nearly a single room. To wager that you could kill someone, and with blows from a solid instrument at that, without waking Staś would have been madness. To wager that the victim would succumb without crying out—madness.

Yet it's hard to imagine such madness overtaking Gorgonowa, a very normal and sober-minded woman. What happened that night? Were these cozy rooms stalked by a provincial Lady Macbeth with a candle, wiping the blood from her hands?

This house is haunted even in broad daylight, even with people here. Haunted not just by the corpse of a girl, but also by the tragic figure of a woman buried alive. Haunted by wicked people, haunted by a grim, petty bourgeois life that has curdled.

Krzywicka observes the site visit through the living room window with the other journalists, who aren't allowed inside.

The interior of the villa is lit with kerosene lamps. Gentlemen in judicial robes have taken seats along the dining room table, looking strange against the background of this bourgeois interior. People are crowded by the window; it's hard to squeeze through. I saw Staś through the glass as he reenacted getting out of bed and all his other movements at the time of the crime. He knocked on the French doors leading from the dining room to the foyer, ran through the foyer, burst into his sister's room—his pace always enormously accelerated, improbable, unreal.

Staś's actions probably took much, much longer than calculated by a stopwatch in the hand. Everyone watching this boy race around the rooms could see that this is not how someone behaves when he's freshly awakened, surprised, frightened, panicking.

Yet if Staś's actions did not take fifteen seconds or so, which seems impossible to me, but rather several minutes, then what was Gorgonowa doing in the garden during this time? Why only after such a significant period did Staś hear the smash of the broken windowpane?

If Staś heard that smash, as he says, while he was running to his father's room, then he should have found her fiddling with the porch door, not by the bed.

No, none of this holds water, I thought, standing on tiptoe, peering from deep in the evening darkness into the illuminated window of the dining room. The boy's face was calm and motionless, repeating all of his movements several times on command.

But wouldn't mentally placing himself back in that horrid night, wouldn't this whole little comic performance have easily strained his nerves? He who bawled like a spoiled child when the defense counsel told him he was giving biased testimony. Here his eyes were dry; he executed everything competently and coherently, oddly coherently and competently if we consider that a year and a half ago he was still a child, and now he is acting out real, tragic events in front of strangers.

I looked from outside at his pale but calm face blinking in and out of sight along the windowpanes. He made gestures when Professor Olbrycht, the main director of this performance, called out in a stentorian voice: "Lusia's been murdered!" He didn't get mixed up, he didn't cry, he didn't refuse this horrible demonstration. This boy has strong nerves.

After a moment, in the background of the window-pane, a second specter appears. Mr. Zaremba with his bald pate, lumpy all over, his face insufficiently materialized, not fully emerged from a mass of flesh and fat.

Oh, he played his role with an actor's precision. In the doorway of his daughter's bedroom he wiped his brow, made gestures of despair, everything at an equally dizzying pace to Staś.

Against the background of the dark alcove of this once-bloodied room, this figure acted out hasty and second-rate despair.

Once it's completely dark, the most important experiment takes place.

A throng of people crowd the little house: the judicial authorities, the police, the press. They turn out the light for a quarter of an hour, so the observers' eyes can adjust to the murk. Flickering in the distance is the little light of the electric bulb at the military-police outpost that allegedly illuminated the figure Staś saw. They are going to check whether Staś could have made out and recognized this mysterious form in the foyer.

During this experiment, Krzywicka stands in Lusia's room. Gorgonowa is a few steps away from her in the foyer.

At a signal, she'll move behind the specially placed Christmas tree, then disappear through the door. They are having her act out a scene in which, according to her assurances, she never took part. Her life may depend on the results of this show.

We all sit motionless and quiet. Darkness. Silence. A cool puff of air on the face. Someone's sigh.

How is it possible to kill in such darkness? How could you strike so accurately?

The minutes go by. We can't see anything.

Maybe Gorgonowa will crack under this pressure, maybe she'll scream, confess?

Does Staś not feel an icy tingle down his back? Maybe he'll cry like a baby and say out loud, maybe shout: "Leave me alone. I don't want to."

It may be that a site visit like this is necessary and will explain many details, but there is a cruelty in it against which human nature rebels. This stagecraft of recalling the crime, this reenactment of it by the people directly involved—is a terrible danse macabre.

The fifteen minutes are up.

On command, Gorgonowa moves through the agreed space. Staś says slowly, calmly: "I think I can see . . ."

Nothing can be seen. Nothing. Not only can one not recognize a person, one cannot even see the outline of their figure. People and objects vanish into the darkness—thick and impenetrable darkness.

On the night of the tragedy there apparently was snow. Even if it had been a little brighter, there would still have been no way of recognizing anything.

Staś could not have seen anything. Staś did not see anything.

THE RESEARCHER VERSUS THE PRACTITIONER

Kraków, Friday, April 21, 1933

A key moment in the Kraków trial is a duel of two professors: an outstanding researcher versus an outstanding practitioner. Warsaw versus Kraków. The government Institute of Hygiene versus the university Department of Forensic Medicine.

Professor Ludwik Hirszfeld, discoverer of the law of heritability of blood types and the person who introduced to world medicine the designations O, A, B and AB, used in criminal investigations all over the world, clashes with Professor Jan Olbrycht, who was the first forensic medical examiner to use Hirszfeld's discovery in criminal cases and to establish disputed paternity.

Their fundamental dispute comes down to the white, bloody handkerchief belonging to Gorgonowa and found in the basement of the house in Brzuchowice. Olbrycht has claimed it has traces of Lusia's blood on it, settling Gorgonowa's guilt—and Hirszfeld claims the exact opposite.

During the trial, Irena Krzywicka makes friends with Professor Hirszfeld because, like her, he's defending Gorgonowa. This sympathy is visible in the articles she writes.

This is how she describes the duel:

We have seen: the leonine head and bald pate, the young face of Professor Hirszfeld squaring off against the Habsburgian profile of Professor Olbrycht. The clash of these two individuals was passionate.

Even before Professor Hirszfeld appeared at the trial, Professor Olbrycht managed to focus attention on himself. Each word he spoke was a pillar propping up the indictment.

Professor Olbrycht behaved as though he could see everything himself. He spoke fluently and confidently, he had no trouble keeping the courtroom riveted. He brought along various apparatuses and demonstrated rather mysterious experiments to the dazzled jurors.

He showed them photographs of blood spectra, surely difficult even for specialists to analyze.

Those in the courtroom might have been inclined to conclude that this is precisely how true science speaks, with such indisputable certitude, equipped for prestige with a stunning prop-shop of scientific instruments—if not for the arrival of Professor Hirszfeld, if not for his testimony.

Professor Hirszfeld is one of the most outstanding scholars in the world. (We should not be surprised if one day he's awarded the Nobel Prize.)

His appearance at the trial became a sensation. (Professor Olbrycht was not thrown off, he gave no deference to his brilliant colleague, he showed him no courtesy.)

[Olbrycht] was acerbic, ironic, biting. He cautioned him good-naturedly, gave advice, notes. He smiled mockingly.

Hirszfeld looked at him with clear, surprised eyes, he did not respond, he did not polemicize. He did not let anger get the better of him.

Rarely have I ever heard anything equally as beautiful as Hirszfeld's testimony. Full of deep modesty, of courtesy toward his tactless opponent, full of noble skepticism. In this speech there was human simplicity, there was elegance, there was sensitive, generous caution. This is exactly how a true scholar should speak.

The professor's personality meant he commanded everyone's attention. His words stripped every ounce of evidentiary significance from the handkerchief from the basement.

Professor Olbrycht's testimony following the scholar from Warsaw made a painful impression: it floundered in schoolboy acerbity, it cited some discussions or other, gave advice and cautions, standing fast by his accusation, because one couldn't possibly call his testimony anything else.

THREE MASTERPIECES

Kraków, Saturday, April 29, 1933

The last day of the trial. After sixteen days of courtroom debate and questioning of experts and witnesses, not much more is known than after last year's trial in Lwów. There has been no breakthrough in the evidence; if anything, it's weaker.

The defense is aiming first and foremost to demonstrate the defendant's total innocence, or at least claim that she committed the crime in a state of insanity, that she was driven to kill by extremely difficult circumstances. And the defense tries to lay the blame for these difficult conditions on Zaremba. It makes him out to be a soulless monster doing his utmost to crudely dispose of the beautiful governess, now that he had taken advantage of her and grown bored with her. "The statements by Gorgonowa's defense were three masterpieces," writes Krzywicka.

> They should remain classic orations in Polish criminology, Polish law. If among us there exists true devotion to speech and talent, they should be printed, so as not to sink into the deaf walls of the courtroom,

having echoed helplessly off the indifferent person-
ages of the gentlemen of the jury. As I was listening,
I regretted the passing of every sentence, every word.
Those marvelous fireworks of talent, wit, emotion,
and thought burst and burned out.

Every blow struck empty air, nothing, zero.

Interest in the trial is enormous. Every newspaper prints ma-
ny-paged transcripts of each sitting, from the nationalist *Nowiny
Codzienne* to the centrist *Ilustrowany Kurier Codzienny* to tabloids like
Łódź's *Express Wieczorny Ilustrowany*. The editors of *Ilustrowany Kurier Codzienny* have announced a special edition of the paper as soon as
the verdict is declared; since late afternoon, several thousand people
have been waiting out in front of the Press Palace on the corner of
Starowiślna Street and Wielopole Street to get their hands on it.

At 7:10 P.M., the judges enter the courtroom for the last time to
read out the verdict. At the press table, Irena Krzywicka writes:

The two-story, gloomy courtroom. Words go dull and
life deadens. Crowding, fever, anticipation. We no
longer hear the words that for two months have been
repeated unto stupefaction: ice-axe, handkerchief,
windowpane, type A, type O. Finished are the shameful interrogation of witnesses, the tragicomic squab-
bles of scholars, finished are the insipid investigations
of things we will never know for certain.

Amid these great judicial maneuvers, the defendant has been forgotten, and now, a moment before
the verdict is announced, no one looks at her. Now
it's about betting: Will they convict? Acquit? In the
home stretch, the defense is three laps ahead of the

prosecution. But this is not a race where victory is explicit. It is a game of chance; it is heads or tails.

The twelve gentlemen of the jury sit with frozen faces. What do they think? What do they feel? And do they at all . . . ?

The gentlemen of the jury receive questions. The gentlemen of the jury come back, asking, unsatisfied, for a larger number of questions. The gentlemen of the jury come back yet again because they don't understand the questions. The gentlemen of the jury come back a third time and proceed to announce the verdict.

The defendant shivers in her fur coat. The lawyers go pale. The public sits stock-still.

Presiding Judge Jendl reads out the verdict:

The defendant Gorgonowa, Emilia Margarita (two given names) is guilty of killing the late Elżbieta Zarembianka in Łączki on the night of December thirtieth to thirty-first, 1931, deliberately and under the influence of strong emotion, having struck her multiple times on the head with a solid instrument. The judge sentences her to imprisonment for a term of eight years.

Krzywicka is upset. She writes:

I cannot resist my confidence in her innocence. Her guilt seems to me too absurd and improbable. The sentence is so mediocre. For after all, it is very, very possible that this woman is innocent. Eight years is not the death penalty some find revolting. Eight years is not the acquittal that sends some into a rage. Do many people serve eight years in prison?

Mr. Jendl is glad. The gentlemen of the jury are glad. They will finally stop talking about this Gorgonowa, of whom everyone is now sick and tired.

But there are people who will find this verdict difficult to accept. Public opinion, soothed by a lightened punishment, has not fully grasped that we still face the question: and what if Gorgonowa is innocent? Then the desperation of this verdict can be nothing but terrifying. We must defend the law that the innocent must not be condemned, that even one day served by an innocent person is a grave memento for the court.

Better to let ten who are guilty walk free than to condemn one who is innocent.

Half a century later, she wrote bluntly in her memoirs:

Defending Gorgonowa was for a lawyer or, equally, a judicial expert or journalist a risky thing. The incredible collective hysteria, stoked by part of the press, which was profiting off of it, and also by part of right-wing public opinion, could be dangerous. (It's a shame I no longer have the poison-pen letters that faithfully reflected the climate of that period and the atmosphere that accompanied the case.)

A CRY OF DESPAIR

Krzywicka interviews Gorgonowa for the only time when, after a day in court, she sits down next to her in the dock. She asks how she finds the strength to carry on through all of this.

"I don't care anymore, I just want to get it over with," the accused replies. "Do you think I still care about my life after all this? If not for my baby . . . But they'll take her away from me too. I'm like a bitch. I have babies and strangers take them away. Zaremba won't let me see Romusia, supposedly because I'm in jail. But when he was in jail he had her brought to him. Did you hear the testimony he gave? Six years I lived with him, two children, four abortions . . . I wish at least he wouldn't lie so brazenly. Other people can say what they want. I couldn't listen to what he was saying."

Krzywicka asks:

"Don't you suspect anyone? Does no one come to mind?"

"How can I suspect anyone?" Gorgonowa replies. "Why, I think I know best of all what it means to suspect without guilt. I know it wasn't me. That is all I know, ma'am."

"I still tremble at the memory of those words and that tone, which could not possibly have been a lie," she writes. "I shake all over when I see her gaze before me and hear her voice, in which I do not cease to sense the truth. I believe her that she was not lying, and I believe myself that if it were a lie, I would sense it.

"That cry of despair will follow me for the rest of my life."

Rita Gorgonowa during the second site visit in Brzuchowice, March 18–19, 1933.

Ilustrowany Tygodnik Kryminalno Sądowy

Rk II. Nr. 2 (52) Cena 30 gr., w Czechosłowacji 1·20 Kc. Wychodzi w każdą niedzielę. 16 str. druku. 10 stycznia 193.

Tajny DETEKTYW

ZBRODNIA W BRZUCHOWICACH.

...odzina inż. Zaremby, zgromadzona na tarasie jego willi w Brzuchowicach. Szczegóły na str. 8—9 i 10.

...ąca od lewej: Staś Zaremba, Rita Gorgonowa ...

Staś Zaremba, Rita Gorgonowa with daughter Romusia, and Lusia on the terrace of the villa in Brzuchowice. This is the first photograph of Gorgonowa to appear in the Polish press.

pokój denatki pozbrodni

Lusia's pink room. Photograph taken after removing her body.

Journalists from *Tajny Detektyw* conduct their own investigation to explain the circumstances of Lusia Zaremba's death. They contact witnesses, get inside the villa, propose hypotheses.

Zaremba, Gorgonowa, and Zaremba's clerk on the balcony of Zaremba's former architectural studio on Hetmańska Street in Lwów.

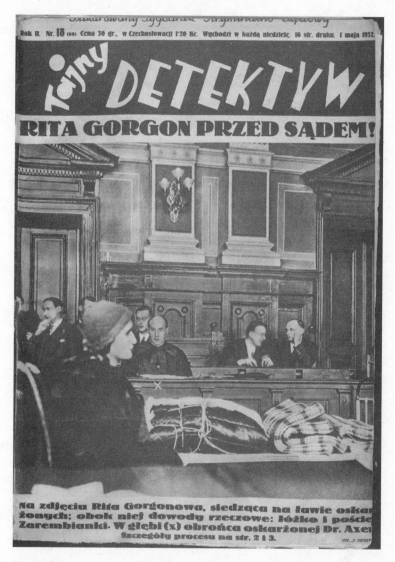

The trial in Lwów; in the background, Gorgonowa's defense counsel Maurycy Axer.

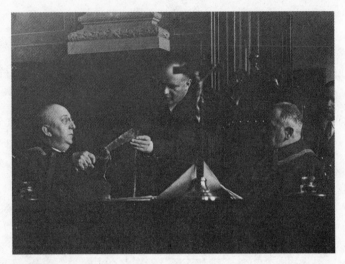

Judges Sylwester Łyczkowski (first from left) and Jan Antoniewicz (first from right) examine the ice-axe during the trial.

Report from the trial in Lwów. In the foreground with his back turned, Staś Zaremba. At the bottom of the page, the witnesses: from left, the servant Bronisława Beckerówna, the gardener's wife, Rozalia Kamińska, the maid Marcelina Tobiaszówna, the neighbor and radio technician Kazimierz Matula, the gardener Józef Kamiński, the artist Czajkowski.

The expert witnesses. Front, from the left: Prof. Jan Opieński and Prof. Antoni Westfalewicz. Back, from the left: Prof. Józef Dadlez and Dr. Karol Piro.

Elga Kern, Polskie Radio broadcast studio in Wilno. Kern is giving a lecture on the need for German-Polish cultural rapprochement. 1931.

Mieczysław Ettinger (right) and Maurycy Axer during the appeal (Warsaw, July 21, 1932).

Rita Gorgonowa's second hearing before the Supreme Court in Warsaw. Visible here, inter alia: Justices Stanisław Wyrobek, Konstanty Syromiatnikow, Presiding Judge Jan Przymowski, Prosecutor Stanisław Błoński, Sept 22, 1933.

The defendant Rita Gorgonowa speaks with her representatives during a break in the proceedings at the District Court in Kraków: Józef Woźniakowski (seated, second from the right) and Mieczysław Ettinger (seated, first from the right).

Kraków citizens in front of the *Ilustrowany Kurier Codzienny* offices at 1 Wielopole Street. The latest news from the courtroom is posted in display cases in front of the building.

The jury box during the trial.

Site visit in Brzuchowice. Seated, from the left: Clerk of the Court Ehrenpreis, Judges Leonard Solecki, Alfred Jendl, Leonard Krupiński, and Jan Ostręga. Brzuchowice, March 18–19, 1933.

Irena Krzywicka

During a site visit with Rita Gorgonowa present. Visible, inter alia: Judge Leonard Solecki (on the left, in the bowler hat and light-colored scarf), Attorney Józef Woźniakowski (right, in the light-colored suit), Prosecutor Bohdan Szypuła (in the light-colored hat and glasses). Brzuchowice, March 18–19, 1933.

Expert witnesses Professor Ludwik Hirszfeld (right) and Professor Jan Olbrycht (left).

The conclusion of the Kraków trial. Gorgonowa sentenced to eight years in prison.

St. Michael's Prison in Kraków. Rita Gorgonowa with her daughter Ewa, 1933.

St. Michael's Prison in Kraków. Gorgonowa with her daughter Ewa in the prison yard, 1933.

Ewa Ilić with her daughter Margarita Ilić-Lisowska.

The archive of Ewa Ilić. A photo of her father Henryk Zaremba, Ewa Ilić as a young woman and her mother Rita Gorgonowa.

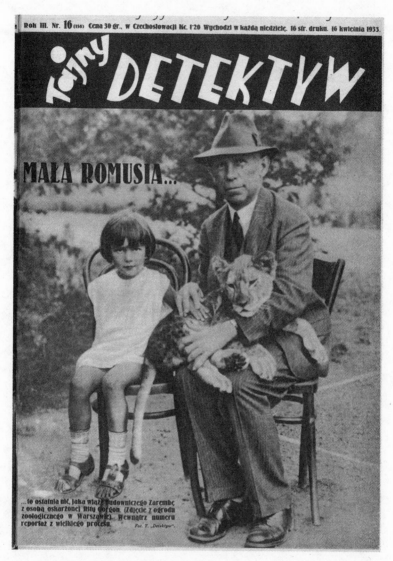

Romusia with her father, Henryk Zaremba.

After moving to Warsaw, Henryk Zaremba legally changed his daughter's name and date of birth, to make her harder to find. She stopped being Romusia. For eighty years she's been Aldona, for sixty, she's had the last name K.

PART II

2016–2017

BRANDED

I know everything about her. That she was born on a Tuesday at 2:30 A.M., that she weighed three kilos, had blond hair, and looked healthy. When her mother went into labor, it set off a frenzy of activity. The chief even had someone call in an obstetrician-gynecologist from the city, but he arrived too late, just as Wagnerowa—serving time for illegal abortions—was delivering the baby.

I know that on September 20, 1932, the whole prison on Kazimierzowska Street was celebrating her birth. And only her mother was sad. She wept and said:

"A child born behind bars will be branded for her whole life."

I know that her arrival saved her mother's life. That's what the evening papers said. But the serious press also devoted a great deal of space to the event. *Ilustrowany Kurier Codzienny*, the most important newspaper of interwar Poland, placed the news of her birth between a note about the largest airship in the world (248 meters long) under construction in Friedrichshafen, Germany, and the boasts of Captain Stanisław Karpiński that he could definitely fly a light aircraft solo across the enormous distance between Poland to Afghanistan (and back).

The first articles about Ewa come out in April 1932. Six months before her birth, details leak to the press about her mother's gyneco-

175

logical exam. Every newspaper in Lwów writes about the pregnancy, reassuring their readers that the baby is in no danger: according to the Penal Code, in such cases a mother is executed only after she gives birth.

She was a much-anticipated baby. The largest newspaper publishers—in Lwów, Warsaw, Kraków, Łódź—couldn't wait for her to be born. They predicted that once interest in her mother had faded, their readers would refocus their attention on the girl and she would pump up their sales.

This means that today we can precisely recreate the first years in the life of Krystyna Ewa Ilić, the daughter of Margarita Gorgonowa and Henryk Zaremba, who for his whole life denied his paternity.

"I don't believe," he writes in his book, "that I have a child with that murderous woman, conceived at a time when she was already thinking of slaying my rightful, sure child. That is her child. I don't know whom she had it with. And I don't want to know."

The question of paternity is not simple to resolve. At the moment of Krystyna Ewa's birth, Rita is formally the wife of Erwin Gorgon, resident in the United States. Her husband could not be the baby's father, while Zaremba has sworn he isn't either. The pre-war Civil Code did not foresee anomalous cases like this one. Therefore on her birth certificate, the girl is given her mother's maiden name—Ilić.

To change it, her mother must prove in court that Zaremba is the baby's father. This is a long and winding road. Since Krystyna Ewa is a minor, the attorney Maurycy Axer fights on her behalf.

A ruling doesn't come until five years later. On June 9, 1937, a Lwów court recognizes Zaremba as the girl's father and orders him to pay child support of eighty złotys a month (retroactive to May 1934).

This changes little in Krystyna Ewa's life because her father doesn't want to know her. He has never considered her his daughter.

He has never hugged her, never visited her in the orphanage, never spoken to her.

Brygidki Prison in Lwów, St. Michael's Prison in Kraków, the Women's Penal Facility in the Fordon district of Bydgoszcz—these are her first family homes.

In Fordon, she lives with her mother on the second floor in a cell for prisoners with small children.

"All the children here are very appreciated. They are like little rays of sunlight cutting through the darkness for the women imprisoned here," writes *Tajny Detektyw*.

But her mother is not appreciated. She's argumentative. Neither the prisoners nor the guards can stand her.

The regulations say Ewa can only stay in the prison for a year. During that time her mother searches for a foster family for her. She writes letters to acquaintances, friends, her husband's family. She asks them to take care of her beloved daughter. When she gets no response, Maurycy Axer takes matters into his own hands. He becomes Ewa's guardian and in September 1933, he sends his secretary to the prison in Fordon. She is to collect the child and in utmost secrecy transport her to Lwów. Ewa ends up in an orphanage on the outskirts of the city. The building on Kadecka Street is adjacent to the Abramowicz Home for developmentally disabled children. Nearby are Lwów's recreational parks and the stadiums of the city's two sports powerhouses: Pogoń and Sokół. Four hundred children live in the orphanage, but only Ewa's presence is a closely guarded secret.

Fearing nosy journalists, the nuns prohibit giving out information about their best-known ward. In particular, they ban showing strangers the way to the room where the girl lives.

"She is guarded as if some sort of attack were planned on this innocent child," writes *Tajny Detektyw*, whose reporter, after several months of searching, discovers where Ewa is hiding and goes to see the girl.

"She has beautiful black eyes, she nearly always smiles and rarely cries," he writes.

Years later, Ewa will remember strangers bringing boxes of chocolate and toys to the orphanage for her. The nuns come and call her from the room, then lead her down the large staircase to the reception room, where visitors are waiting for her. They bring presents and don't want anything from her. She feels special. Yet in time, a feeling of shame bubbles up, once she realizes they look at her like some little animal. Once she's learned to speak, her older friends explain to her why this is going on. That day is etched on her memory. She goes into the large, sunlit playroom. The children stop their games, start to surround her, stand in a tight little circle and point their fingers at her, shouting: "Nasty Gorgon, nasty Gorgon, nasty Gorgon!"

One asks:

"Did your mother kill Lusia?"

Ewa doesn't know who Lusia is. She doesn't know how to respond. She just angrily throws her blocks on the floor.

From then on, she'll always defend her mother. Once she learns to clench her fists, she'll fling them at girls who call her "nasty Gorgon." The nuns are very strict, and every time she does, they punish her by locking her in a cell under the stairs overnight with a pig.

(In time she'll understand that this epithet is the worst insult, and that there is no defense against it.)

When she was three, maybe four, the nuns came for her at night in the convent. They took her downstairs, put her in a carriage, and took her to the main train station in Lwów. She left on her first train ride, a long journey to a strange city, on whose outskirts stood a grim, concrete edifice. She followed the nuns down murky corridors and went through grated gates, until she reached a steel door, which a man in a gray uniform opened with a large key.

She remembers seeing a sad woman on a cot.

"This is your mama," a nun said to her, and pushed her into the woman's arms.

She later talked about this meeting in interviews: "I wanted so badly for her to hug me. But she didn't know how. As if someone had frozen her in ice, turned her into a living statue. She looked me in the eye. For a long time, with excruciating sadness. And definitely with love because, after all, a mother loves her child."

She can't remember her face. She only remembers the warmth of her body. And that it was a one-person cell, she thinks, because she doesn't remember other prisoners.

After returning to Lwów, Ewa will send childish drawings to her: a house, a tree, the sun.

Her mother writes in copying pencil on gray paper. The nuns always read the letters to Ewa before she goes to sleep. Her mother writes that she loves her little Kropelka very much, that she misses her, and that the girl is her only solace in an unhappy life. In those days, Ewa lives in hope that her mother will come back and free her from the orphanage.

On September 1, 1939, the Germans invade Poland. Three weeks later, the Soviets are already outside Lwów. Panic breaks out in the city. Rumors fly that the Bolsheviks will burn down churches and rape nuns. The sisters from the orphanage jettison their habits, take the crosses off the walls and the saints' medals from around the children's necks. This is how Ewa loses her final memento of her mother—a small gold medal of the Blessed Virgin with the archangels, which until now she has worn around her neck.

The children spend entire days in the cellars of the orphanage on Kadecka, praying for rescue. The nuns warn them that the Bolsheviks will tear out the tongue of anyone who confesses faith in God. But the Soviets don't harm the children. They even bring treats for them: potatoes and salted fish. The repressions fall on the Polish intelligentsia and Lwów's military defenders: the former are exiled to Siberia, the latter are executed at Katyn.

Famine comes two years later, when the Germans invade the USSR. After entering Lwów, the Wehrmacht sets up its barracks in the orphanage on Kadecka. That night, military trucks drive up to the building. The nuns lead the children out down one set of stairs, while the Germans move in up the other.

Ewa will remember her last meal on Kadecka. Polenta with black weevils in it. Later they didn't even have that.

After their eviction from the orphanage the children face hunger. Every day, Ewa slips into the German barracks through a hole in the fence and waits under a window until the soldiers throw out the scraps from the garrison kitchen. There she can find bones to chew on, if she moves faster than the hungry dogs.

She's ten in 1942, when the nuns pile all their wards into a truck and take them nearly 250 kilometers west to Tarnów, to a convent of the Little Servant Sisters of the Immaculate Conception.

In Tarnów they call them "the Lwów girls" and make fun of their sing-song accents. There are twenty of them. They infect the Tarnów girls with their antipathy for Nasty Gorgon.

The children tease her, but she beats them up. The nuns consider her a troublemaker. She doesn't want to pray. She often ends up in solitary confinement in the basement. They tell her to kneel and rattle off Hail Marys, rosaries, the hours. It's no help. The moment someone turns up who's willing to take her in, the orphanage quickly gets rid of her.

Ewa ends up with two spinster sisters. They need her for cheap labor. She's meant to call the older one "Auntie." The younger is a little infirm. They live in the countryside with their old, desiccated, sickly mother, who is constantly jolted by convulsions.

The girl plows, reaps, threshes, grinds. She cleans, cooks, brings brushwood from the forest and water from the well. Always in the same old, torn dress "Auntie" picked out for her from clothes left behind by deported Jews. She's always hungry. ("Auntie" is very stingy and skimps on food.) When Ewa's really hungry, she sneaks into the pigsty and picks out potatoes from the trough. She doesn't even have a bed. She sleeps on a bundle of hay in the attic.

Ewa doesn't remember the Germans retreating. Maybe because nothing changed. She can't go to school because Auntie says it's not for her. Nor is she allowed to read books. She's supposed to be a farmhand.

Luckily, the principal of the local school tells her to enroll. He's even bought her a dress, a winter coat, and shoes. She's thirteen and is immediately placed in third grade.

She's a good student and that saves her. When she finishes elementary school, she goes off to a vocational school in Częstochowa. There she lives in a dormitory with other orphans. Three days of school, three days of work in the textile factory. She becomes a spinner and can now support herself.

In the late 1940s she begins to search for her mother, fruitlessly.

She has no intention of looking for her father. (This is how she talks about him: "After what he did to me and Mama, he's nobody to me.")

Nevertheless, the head of the nursing school in Wrocław, where Ewa enrolls in 1954, encourages her to find her father and go to court for child support.

She even wants to—to stand before him, look him in the eye, and ask: "Why did you disown me?"

Only it's too late. She learns Zaremba's in a hospital in Warsaw. He's gravely ill. He dies of a heart attack on June 26, 1954.

FOLLOWING LEADS: IN SEARCH OF AN
ALTERNATE VERSION OF EVENTS

As early as January 1932, reporters from the Kraków weekly magazine *Tajny Detektyw* are trying to solve the mystery of Lusia's murder. They travel to Brzuchowice, talk with neighbors and witnesses. They reconstruct the course of events. They search for an alternate version. Unlike the investigators, they take as their working hypothesis that the killer wasn't Gorgonowa but a stranger who forced his way into the garden at night, broke into the house, murdered Lusia, and fled.

And why did he leave no footprints on the fresh snow? There's an explanation for that too: they were filled in by a blizzard that blew through Brzuchowice that tragic night. The magazine even gives a precise time for the snowstorm: between 10 P.M. and 1 A.M.

"If someone made it onto the property during this blizzard, the footprints left by this person must have been filled in completely by the heavy snowfall and would be unnoticeable later for the search party trio: Staś, the gardener, and Sergeant Trela," writes *Tajny Detektyw*.

The magazine concludes that the murderer broke into the villa after the household went to sleep, meaning after 10:45 P.M. He killed Lusia at around 11:15 and escaped through the garden at 11:30 at the latest. That's why when the household searched for the murderer an hour later, they could no longer find his footprints in the snow.

Only this means Lusia's death must have taken place not, as the police investigation hypothesized, right before Staś woke up, but an hour earlier. *Tajny Detektyw* claims this is possible: "Since it was not proved when the killer carried out his dreadful act, we cannot claim it took place directly before Staś was roused from sleep."

Theoretically this is possible, because the Lwów anatomical pathologists did not address the time of death at all in their autopsy. They accepted the determination of Dr. Csala, who was summoned to the Zarembas' house and who at around one in the morning declared that death had taken place very recently.

(In 1933, the Kraków expert witness Professor Jan Olbrycht attempted to precisely determine the time of death based on the documentation he had collected. It was no longer possible. He concluded that the girl's death could have taken place even just after 9:30, when everyone had just gone to bed.)

Tajny Detektyw writes that a psychopath and sexual maniac might have committed the crime, not Gorgonowa. The reporters discover that such a person roamed the area of Hołosko township just after the Great War. He murdered four teenage girls in a radius of barely a few hundred meters from the Zarembas' villa. The last one was the daughter of Sergeant Juśkiewicz from Lwów: she was found dead in 1922 only a hundred meters from Hołosko train station, halfway to the engineer's villa. All these killings were connected by one important detail: before their deaths, each girl's hymen was broken. Hence the reporters propose the fifth victim of this same psychopathic pervert might have been Lusia.

The topic of a psychopathic pervert will be raised again during the trial in Lwów in 1932, when twelve-year-old Józefa Neuwerówna is raped and murdered by an unknown perpetrator. Gorgonowa's defense lawyer, Maurycy Axer, claims that both girls died in a similar fashion, which in his opinion is evidence that a sexual maniac was involved in the killing in Brzuchowice. Yet during the trial, three expert witnesses compare both murders and find few similarities. The main difference is that Neuwerówna was raped while alive, and Zarembianka's staged rape was performed after her death.

In the experts' view, "the perpetrator could not have been the same person."

The hypothesis of a stranger breaking into the house has a serious flaw. Even if someone overcame the ice and snow, forced through the tall fence, dodged the teeth of Lux, the menacing German shepherd who was guarding the yard, and successfully erased their footprints, the question would still remain: How did they get into the locked villa?

Through the thirty-centimeter opening in the vent window in Lusia's room? That was too small for anyone to squeeze through.

Through the bolted porch door? It was impossible to open from the outside and it showed no sign of a break-in.

From the backyard? Through the kitchen door? That was also locked and the servant Marcelina Tobiaszówna was sleeping by it. An oil lamp was burning next to her bed all night long.

Could the intruder have forced the door open so quietly as not to wake her? Would he risk it, seeing the light in the window?

He would have to know the layout of the villa, get past the maid's bed, then go down a narrow, dark hallway to the dining room, slip past Staś sleeping two meters away, open the French doors to the foyer and go into Lusia's room. Would a psychopathic sexual maniac be capable of this? Would he know how to find the bolts in the front door, open them, and escape unnoticed through the garden, past a fearsome dog?

Even supposing an intruder might possess preternatural knowledge, insane bravery, and incredible cunning, allowing him to escape unnoticed through the fence, that leaves the question of whether the snowfall was really so heavy it could have eliminated all traces of his presence in an hour and a half.

The Kraków court researches the intensity of snowfall in Brzucho-wice in 1933, based on data from two weather stations in the area around Lwów. Neither recorded a violent blizzard. The military meteorologists of the air force regiment in Lwów only registered minor snowfall. The weather observatory at Lwów Polytechnic provided similar data. (Both stations were located around ten kilometers from Brzuchowice.)

If we accept it was an intruder who murdered Lusia, who, then, did Staś Zaremba see an hour later, after he woke up? After all, he described fairly precisely a woman in a fur coat in the dark foyer.

Tajny Detektyw, like Elga Kern, thinks this was a hallucination.

> The fact that Staś saw some figure after waking up does not yet prove that this phenomenon was real. People, especially juveniles, do not regain their full awareness of reality just after waking up. The impressions their consciousness receives in this state of mind are often exaggerated or even arise in abstraction. Therefore to claim that Staś saw concretely such-and-such a person is risky. A Christmas tree was standing in the foyer, the room was dark, slightly scattered with reflected light from the white surface of snow. In lighting conditions such as these, it would not be difficult to be deceived!

But as sleepy deceptions go, this figure was very real, for when it slipped through the half-open door, it left such clear footprints on the snow that an hour later they led Sergeant Trela to the porch outside Rita's room. Hallucinations don't leave footprints.

Elga Kern proposes one more hypothesis. It focuses on the basement across from the pool. While the Zarembas were staying in Brzuchowice it was never locked. Kern presumes the attacker could have hidden in it much earlier, before the household went to sleep, and waited there for the right moment to strike. When the lights went out and the conversations died down, he left his hiding place and killed Lusia. He wouldn't have had to break into the house, because an interior staircase led from the basement all the way up to the attic. He could have taken it up to Lusia's room. The door was right near the girl's bed.

Theoretically this would be possible. The investigators looked into this suggestion as well. On the day of the killing, the internal staircase was blocked with junk and it would have been impossible to get up it without making a lot of noise. And even if someone managed to, the next barrier would be the door to Lusia's room itself. It was locked, covered with a kilim, and blocked off with a linen chest. There was no chance of opening it without awakening the household.

And so, from the very beginning the investigators' main hypothesis is that a member of the household murdered Zarembianka. The theory of a killer breaking in from outside is so unlikely that even Gorgonowa's defense team doesn't attempt to exploit it further. They prefer to develop the thesis that someone inside the house committed the murder. Except they deny, of course, that it was their client.

But if not Gorgonowa, then who?

NASTY GORGON

"A sweet, pleasant young woman, but she lives in the shadow of her notoriety and is attempting to escape its confines," writes the journalist Czesław Ostańkowicz of the Wrocław weekly *Sygnały*. In 1957, he discovers Gorgonowa's daughter in the small village of Kamionki in Lower Silesia. Ewa is twenty-five years old. She works in the Workers' Vacation Fund rest home. She's a kitchen maid. "Imagine being constantly alone. Always without anyone. With a life story like mine," she explains to the journalist.

> Like every other young woman, I want to have a mother. Is that so strange? She loved me, after all. I can only vaguely remember her face, wet with tears. I used to send drawings I made in the orphanage to her in prison.
>
> I have to find my mother! If only because she's the only one who can tell me the truth about the tragedy in Brzuchowice. I never believed she was the murderer.

Ostańkowicz's article is a parable about a daughter's infinite love for her unknown mother. Ewa, who doesn't even remember what she looked like, searches for her all over the world and bears all the suffering and degradation that fall on her because of the dark legend of her mother.

The tale of the brand that the murderess's daughter wears starts in the late 1940s, in a textile factory in Częstochowa. A colleague at the factory brings seventeen-year-old Ewa a pre-war pamphlet about the Gorgonowa case. From it the girl learns for the first time what happened in Brzuchowice. She's stunned. She's afraid she'll be recognized. So she quits her job in the factory and flees to Wrocław. She goes to nursing school and does a residency at a hospital in the nearby town of Dzierżoniów. On one of her shifts there, something very unpleasant happens.

As she's bringing a boy a glass of medicine, a woman she doesn't know runs up to her and cries:

"I won't have my son getting his medication from a murderer's daughter!"

Ewa never goes back to the hospital. She goes to another town, Pieszyce.

She works as a dental assistant in a health clinic. She meets a nice boy and they fall in love. Her fiancé is progressive, so when Ewa confides in him about her darkest secret, he only shrugs. "There's no way you could blame a daughter for her mother's crime," he replies. He just asks her not to mention it to his mother, who's less open-minded. The couple keep their secret until the Thaw of 1956. Then Poland's most popular magazine, *Po Prostu*, once again tells the story of the murder in Brzuchowice. And once again, all of Poland is interested in Kropelka. Finally Ewa is unmasked.

Her progressive fiancé stops coming to visit. People in Pieszyce say she's inherited her mother's bad reputation and might even strangle her own baby without premeditation because she has it in her blood.

When Ostańkowicz finds her at the vacation home in Kamionki, she tells him ruefully:

"It's quiet here. People go off home after their two-week vacation and don't have time to care about the identity of a kitchen maid they met. They definitely don't mention the Gorgonowa case to me. Unless everything changes after your article. Maybe I'll be as famous again as I was when my friends used to read out the revelations about Kropelka? Maybe they'll whisper again that that's me—the daughter of Lusia's killer?"

Czesław Ostańkowicz's article changes Ewa's life.

In November 1957, it's reprinted by the very popular monthly, *Magazyn Polski*. Everyone learns about Ewa, holed up in Kamionki. All of Poland, even the entire world: *Magazyn Polski* also reaches large communities of Polish emigrants in Africa, Europe, Australia, and both Americas. One person moved by the fate of Gorgonowa's daughter is a Polish émigré in the United States, Józef K., who sends her a letter with words of support and money in dollars.

Soon he falls in love with Ewa and invites her to America. But before she can go, a telegram from Warsaw arrives in Kamionki: "I've found you. I'm looking for Mother, without success. Your sister Roma."

Ewa is euphoric after finding her older sister. She packs a bundle and travels to Warsaw. Romusia is twenty-nine. She lives with her engineer husband and seven-year-old daughter, Grażynka, near the train station in a newly constructed apartment building on Nowolipki Street.

Ewa sees her sister for the first time when the door of Roma's apartment opens a crack. She looks a little like her, but shorter. She has dark hair and their father's blue eyes.

The apartment is cramped. Romusia's family is crowded into one little room. The second, larger one is occupied by the apartment's co-owner.

In the evening Romusia sets up a fold-out cot for her sister in the shared room and asks her to stay longer. At first it's like a fairy tale.

CEZARY ŁAZAREWICZ

The sisters are taken with one another; they get acquainted, discover, and love each other, while they live together in a room of twelve square meters.

The more they love each other, the more they talk about their parents. Ewa defends her mother, and Romusia, her father. Who was more guilty, who betrayed whom? The quarrels grow louder, more brutal. A mutual hostility emerges: Ewa toward Roma, Roma toward Rita, Ewa toward their father. By the end of a year together they're no longer on speaking terms.

Józef from America also loses interest in Ewa. He withdraws his invitation to the United States. In his farewell he writes he learned terrible things about her in a letter from Poland. Ewa suspects Romusia of going behind her back and moves out of Nowolipki. Rather than traveling to America, she goes to the town of Trzebiatów, near the Baltic coast. There, in 1966, she has her only daughter—named Margarita, after her grandmother. As a single mother, the town authorities give Ewa a cubbyhole in the attic of an ex-German tenement. Tiny, dark, and windowless. This is the first apartment she has to herself.

In 1977, Janusz Majewski's movie *The Gorgonowa Case* arrives on the Polish silver screen. The film precisely recreates the night of December 30–31, 1931 and the trials in Lwów and in Kraków, but makes no determination of guilt. Instead, Majewski focuses on the doubts, showing the lack of hard evidence in the case. And since there was no proof, no one can be convicted—that's the film's most important message. Ewa sees *The Gorgonowa Case* for the first time in the Morskie Oko movie theater in Trzebiatów. Her closest family appears on the screen. Her mother has the face of the actress Ewa Dałkowska, and her father, the features of Roman Wilhelmi. In the movie, Staś is gentle, and Lusia quick-witted.

When Ewa sees on screen how her mother was treated after her arrest, tears run down her cheeks. No one in the theater in Trzebiatów knows why.

And once again, journalists are interested in her. They're looking for her to find out what she thinks.

Edmund Żurek from the magazine *Prawo i Życie* comes to her attic apartment with a bouquet of flowers. "I was born in prison, I've lived without a mother or father, without loved ones or relatives, without a home, branded horribly as the daughter of a murderess," she says, telling him her story.

> For years and years I've felt like an animal, chased away, beaten, hungry. Born in prison, the daughter of a woman sentenced to death, I ought to die behind bars or on a trash heap. But a person can carry the weight of life, even if it's beyond her strength.

"Ewa doesn't believe her mother is guilty," notes Żurek, and he quotes her most important argument: "Rita Gorgonowa never hit a child, so how could she have killed seventeen-year-old Lusia, whom she'd cared for, and done it in such a cruel, devious, shameful way?"

FOLLOWING LEADS: IN LVIV

Lychakiv Cemetery, section 53, next to the red sandstone vault of the Kubajewicz-Szczerb family. Elżbieta Zarembianka's grave lies on the right side of the path leading to the cemetery of the Lwów Eaglets. Modest. Undecorated. It is a mound of earth surrounded by a concrete frame with a cross of welded metal tubes set into it. On the cross hangs the same pre-war white plaque, referring to her as an innocent victim of murder. Burned-out grave lanterns and artificial flowers tied together with a red-and-white ribbon. A sign that someone comes here sometimes.

The cemetery office doesn't know who visits Lusia's grave, who lays flowers and lights grave lanterns. The grave is sure to remain permanently because the cemetery is now historically preserved.

My first impressions of Lviv: everything is very close together. To walk from the front of the Bernardines' Church, where the procession with Zarembianka's coffin set off, to the Palace of Justice, where the court sentenced Gorgonowa to death, you need only cross Halytska Square, turn left, and before you is Kniaz Roman (formerly Batory) Street. Beneath three large windows on the second floor, under the pediment with an allegorical sculpture of justice, a crowd of the city's citizens stood in May 1932, demanding Gorgonowa's death.

Now the building holds Lviv Polytechnic National University. The hallway on the second floor looks like the inside of a convent. Herds of Ukrainian students walk down it. In front of the former Courtroom 1, where Gorgonowa's fate hung in the balance, there stands a figure of the Virgin Mary with a wreath of flowers in her hair. The door to the room is padlocked. Peeking through the gap, I see a general renovation is underway, and all that remains of the former courtroom décor is the dark-brown paneling on the walls.

The former Carmelite convent, where the prison was, is located in the courtyard. Apart from Gorgonowa, under Austro-Hungarian rule it held political prisoners who went on to be ministers in independent Poland. "A grim edifice," in the words of the journalists covering the trial. Now corrugated metal garages stand on the site, and the former prison has been converted into a corporate office building.

Nor is it so far to Brygidki Prison (known as Bryhidky in Ukrainian) on Horodotska Street (formerly Kazimierzowska Street). You have to take Svoboda Avenue, past the former Grand Theater. The prison looks like the old photographs in *Tajny Detektyw*. From the front it could still pass for a convent, but when you look at it from the former Karna (now Dmytro Danylyshyn) Street, you can see barbed wire, bars, covered windows, and a sign for the State Penitentiary Service of Ukraine.

In front of the former main gate, where the prisoners were once held, we can read on a metal plaque that here the Soviet NKVD murdered over a thousand Ukrainians, Poles, Jews, and Austrians. But not a word about Gorgonowa. In Lviv her name doesn't conjure up any particular associations. "That mustn't surprise you," writes Irina Pokazanova, a Russian from Lviv who's interested in the Gorgonowa case.

After the war, the population of Lviv underwent a transition: many ethnic Poles left to go to Poland,

and the Jews had been killed. Their place was taken by Russians, who arrived from the east, and Ukrainians from the surrounding villages. The history of Lviv wasn't taught in schools and what happened here in 1939, when the Second World War broke out, our textbooks called "the unification of Ukraine." What came before was rarely mentioned. So how were people supposed to find out about Gorgonowa?

I found Pokazanova online because on her blog she described in great detail the story of the governess from Brzuchowice.

When I asked her why, she writes back from Lviv in Russian:

"It's nothing special. The remarkable, tragic story, and a movie about her I saw. It was necessity. I had to take it on."

From her I know that in Lviv there are no documents, records, files or witnesses who might remember anything. ("You'd have had to look for them long ago, now there's no one left to ask.") Meanwhile, for many months she has been conducting her own private investigation about Brzuchowice (known in Ukrainian as Briukhovychi), and the former Marszałkowska Street, where the Zarembas' villa stood.

This isn't so simple because during the war, the building was devastated—we don't know whether by bombing or by visits from thieves—and then dismantled and looted. Just like many other buildings in Briukhovychi. Where the old houses stood, new ones were built; the layout and names of the streets have been changed. And the last Poles who might have remembered the events of Gorgonowa's story left in the 1970s. Comparing old maps to new ones also gets you nowhere—they don't have points in common and don't line up with one another. Pokazanova searched on. "If you look carefully at photos of the villa from the time of the investigation, there in the background you can see a spot where Soviet Pioneers would later camp out," she writes in another e-mail to me.

Meaning Zaremba's house stood near the Pioneer camp. And a former inhabitant of Briukhovychi told me where that camp was. He told me about walking around in the ruins of Zaremba's villa. Only the foundations remained. But besides that the pool and fountain had survived.

She sends a photograph of a concrete barrack, covered in orange tar paper.

"This is the military police station at 47 Marszałkowska Street. According to a map from 1914 it stood near Zaremba's house," writes Pokazanova, who has recently cracked the whole mystery: "the Polish Marszałkowska Street is the Ukrainian Zapashna Street, and the old number 50, where Zaremba's house was, is now number 8. Zaremba's house was here." She's found it and sends a modern photo.

"In old photographs the villa has a characteristic semicircular wall by the windows, and this house in the photo does too. We can see it was rebuilt on the same foundation. It can't be any other address: only 8 Zapashna Street," she assures me.

Briukhovychi can now only be reached by a marshrutka, a rickety converted Mercedes truck that works as something between an intercity bus and a private taxi. The station for line number 8 is in front of St. Anne's Church in Lviv. It takes fifteen minutes to reach the center of the village.

The town has no rural cabins, farmhouses, makeshift buildings. No women in headscarves sitting on stoops. Everywhere, wealth is plain to see. Varnished shingles, wrought iron gates, mansard roofs, remote-controlled garage doors, and cameras mounted at entrances. Modeled on medieval castles, American mansions, Polish manor houses. Lots of glass, marble, chromed steel. An upmarket suburb with a nouveau-riche lavishness.

Nothing here resembles the streets and homes in the old photos. There's no point of reference.

Nor has anyone here heard of Gorgonowa, Zaremba, Lusia, or the most famous trial of interwar Poland. No one is interested in who lived here before, what the streets were called, which way they went. No one even knows that there used to be a military police station here.

Following Irina's instructions, I go down Zapashna Street. Behind a Soviet-era concrete fence stands a modern, multi-story house with red metal shingles. A massive plot of land with pine trees growing on it. This is where Zaremba's villa stood. Looking through a gap in the fence, I can't see anyone. No one answers the ring of the intercom.

I, RITA'S DAUGHTER

Before I went to Trzebiatów, I found a photo of Ewa online. In 1933 she's a blonde cherub in a white dress in her mother's arms. She looks like a large doll. Her mother stands in the shadow of a large tree next to an elegant man in an old-fashioned suit. This is the Warsaw attorney Mieczysław Ettinger, one of Rita's defense lawyers. He smiles at Ewa, holding her little hand. (The picture was taken on a sunny day in the prison yard.)

A second photo shows gray walls, iron prison cots, and a mother leaning over a metal basin, inside which a little girl smiles at the photographer. This is Ewa.

Eighty-three years later, I climb the stairs to the third floor of an ex-German apartment building; she opens the door and looks at me through thick-lensed glasses.

We sit down by a Christmas tree: the holidays have just ended. A black-and-white photo of her mother with a bouquet of flowers hangs over the TV set. It's the only memento of her. A portrait sent by someone who once read that she couldn't remember her mother at all.

In the papers they still call her "Kropelka," though no one says that to her face anymore. It annoys her that journalists twist everything around and keep asking her the same thing:

"How are you so sure your mother didn't kill her?"

"I just know," she tells *Wprost* magazine. With *Gazeta Wyborcza*, she answers a question with a question: "If I were the child of a murderer, would I have grown up to be a decent person? I had a thousand opportunities to hit rock-bottom and I always pulled through somehow."

Eighty-three-year-old Ewa Ilić's life can be divided into two periods. In the first, she was looking for her mother. In the second, her mother's grave. Today she's closed up her kiosk on the market square, where she sells leather accessories, to tell me about it.

"What I care about is writing as much as possible about how she was innocent and how much harm her sentence did her. I've known it since my earliest years," she explains.

We travel back to 1931. She leads me around the villa, which we both know from the same books, articles, reminiscences. We drift through the yard, through the nooks and crannies of the house, through the foyer where the Christmas tree stood, through the French doors, through the dining room, to her mother's room, and then on to Zaremba's room. We get to know the members of the household and we send young Lusia off to bed. We turn out the light and fall asleep with Ewa's mother. Staś's shout awakens us. We go up to the French doors with him. Zaremba runs into the dining room. And everything starts all over again.

Ewa's daughter, Margarita Ilić-Lisowska, lives in Szczecin; I phoned her before coming to Trzebiatów, and she asked me not to bother her mother too much. She says she finds it hard to pick at the wounds:

"You all take off, and she gets left with it afterward."

So I don't pester her with questions. I sit on a convertible sofa and listen to her talk.

About her unconditional love for a mother she doesn't even remember. About how much she misses her and how incredibly attached she feels to her.

I marvel at how she weaves scraps together into her idealized portrait, without cracks or flaws. And she still resents her father, for leaving her and never lending a helping hand. For the way she got kicked around, demeaned because of him, how she suffered hunger and never knew the warmth of a real home.

"He was a really evil and rotten man," she claims.

She talks about searching for her mother and the life she's dedicated to it. And about her greatest dream, which never came true: to get the chance to hug her.

She's been looking for her for as long as she can remember, ever since she read in a newspaper in the late 1940s that her mother had maybe fled to Yugoslavia. She went to a police station to ask about it, and they arrested her, suspecting she was a spy for Marshal Tito.

She wrote to the public prosecutor's office, to the courts, to the Yugoslav embassy, to the International Red Cross.

She found the Paris address of the writer Irena Krzywicka, who in the 1930s had defended her mother in the pages of *Wiadomości Literackie*.

"For many years I've been searching for you, just like my own mother. I have not found my mother yet. Do you know anything about her?" she asked in her letter.

"I fought for your mother's acquittal in conjunction with Professor Hirszfeld (expert witness) and the lawyers: Axer, Ettinger, and Woźniakowski, sadly in vain, the voice of ignorance was stronger, and then the war," Krzywicka wrote from Paris. But without any concrete information. "What happened to your Mother, I have no idea."

Ewa gave up her search in the 1970s.

"Because everywhere I wrote, they knew nothing about her. It was clear by then that my mother was dead."

"How were you so sure?"

"If she were alive, she'd definitely have found me."

Now she's left with her final dream—before she dies, to clear her mother's name of all charges.

"After what I've learned my whole life, I know my mother was innocent. I know one hundred percent. There was no evidence against her and you can't call her a murderer," she says, exasperated.

She doesn't accept that Staś's testimony incriminated her mother.

"Staś himself was the murderer," she says. "I understood that when I reconstructed in my mind what happened there. I've been thinking about it my whole life. I know it'll set off a firestorm, but that's exactly what happened. It must have been him. And Zaremba knew about it for sure. But why did he have to incriminate my mother to save his own family? That's why now we need a trial to clear my mother and vindicate her. At first my daughter didn't want to deal with it, then she couldn't find a lawyer. A year ago I saw a light at the end of the tunnel because we found a lawyer and he promised to help. I signed the power of attorney agreement and I'm waiting for him to collect evidence and apply to the court to acquit my mother. I'd like to live to see it."

FOLLOWING LEADS: COULD IT HAVE BEEN STAŚ?

In photographs from the first Lwów trial, young Zaremba, in a suit that's a little too big, still looks like an overgrown child. He gives the impression more of a teacher's pet than a delinquent. At the time he's fourteen. Could he have killed his older sister? The question was never posed in the courtroom.

Why would he have done it? After all, they were incredibly close. He looked up to her. She mothered him. She cared for and guided him. The boy had no motive.

And how could such a fragile boy, who sobbed in the courtroom like a baby, have found the strength to commit such an awful crime, erase the evidence, feign indifference, and lie about it for many months? If he had killed her, would he have gotten the whole house out of bed? Why would he have drawn attention to himself? Surely he'd want to make sure not to wake anyone, slip quietly into bed, and wait until morning for someone else to find the body.

Did the investigators of eight decades ago consider the possibility that it might have been him? If they were professionals, then definitely. There is no trace of it in the files. Even the tabloids of the day, spinning the most fantastical speculations, never went as far as to publicly ask whether the brother and sister could have had an incestuous relationship.

If that were the case, we could hypothesize that on the night of the murder, something took place between the siblings in Lusia's room and something sent them out of control, leading to the tragedy. (Yet even then it would be hard to explain why Staś screamed to wake everyone up.)

"So far he's been indifferent to sexual matters," writes the psychologist Dr. Marcin Zieliński, in his court-commissioned expert opinion. He finds that Staś likes being at home and pursuing technical projects, and he's familiar with the workings of a radio. When he gets home from school he plays with mechanical robots he builds himself.

He often prays in church ("Prayer is giving thanks and making requests to God"). He goes regularly to confession ("Sin is a violation of God's law"; "confession is purification from sin").

Shy, embarrassed, phlegmatic, absent-minded, quick to tears— this is how Dr. Zieliński describes him.

Could such a person murder his sister in cold blood?

Dr. Zieliński's expert opinion is very important because it lends credence to the testimony of the main prosecution witness and confirms the boy's excellent memory.

Dr. Zieliński told young Zaremba to memorize strings of numbers and then repeat them on command. Staś passed the test with flying colors. He was able to faultlessly recall six-number combinations even after eight minutes. "This shows the boy has a very good memory," wrote Zieliński.

And one more thing: the psychologist did not claim that his subject had hallucinations. Moreover, he emphasized that the boy remembered precisely what happened right after waking up, because Zieliński tested that, too.

ERASING THE TRACES?

The last administrative trace comes from Sunday, September 3, 1939: a dry judicial note stuck in the files, saying that before completing her full sentence, the condemned left the prison at 1 Młyńska Street in Poznań. She is one of thousands of imprisoned criminals who were freed on an amnesty declared by President Ignacy Mościcki following the German invasion two days prior.

When the prison gates open before her, she's thirty-eight and has three children: twenty-two-year-old Erwinek, taken away by the Gorgon family, eleven-year-old Romusia, taken away by Zaremba, and seven-year-old Krystyna Ewa, taken away by the state. From letters she receives in prison, she knows that Erwinek is seriously sick and in a hospital in Bystra, Silesia. She does not know what's become of her two daughters. She has no money, home, family, or friends. She has nothing but her name—which, everywhere, wherever it appears, causes revulsion.

She can't leave Poznań because the city is on the front line, and soon the Germans take it. The city and its surrounding region are now incorporated into the Greater German Reich as part of the Wartheland. Terror, persecutions, deportations. This is the beginning of the large-scale deportation of a quarter-million Poles from

German-annexed territories and into the military occupation zone known as the General Government.

In January 1940, she's recognized through a prison peephole by a Poznań courthouse guard named Jan Jakubowski. She's sitting on a stool in a cell with her head down ("Black hair, a black pullover, a houndstooth skirt, low-heeled shoes"). When Jakubowski suggests she flee, she firmly refuses:

"There's no rescue for me. I am Gorgonowa," she replies, and withdraws into the depths of the cell.

"Based on the whole event and course of affairs, it's hard to determine whether Gorgonowa remained alive," writes Jan Jakubowski in a letter to the editors of *Prawo i Życie*.

The proof that she did survive comes in a notice headlined "Gorgonowa—Fraud Victim" on the second-to-last page of *Kurier Częstochowski* on Friday, October 18, 1940.

The paper writes of Gorgonowa's visit to a police station in the Powiśle district of Warsaw. She reports the theft of a gold ring worth one hundred złotys. She gives as her place of residence a homeless shelter on Czerniakowska Street.

We don't know how she reached Warsaw, how she was supporting herself, or whether she tried to make it into Soviet-occupied Lwów to look for Ewa there.

In 1941 or 1942, a certain Michał Horoszewicz saw her in court on Warsaw's Leszno Street. Residents of the shelter on Czerniakowska were accusing her of stealing a purse. This trial was also circumstantial. None of these women saw the theft but assumed that Gorgonowa must have done it. Testifying unanimously, they also accused her of spending too much time in the bathroom and causing noise by flushing the lavatory and rustling toilet paper. The court found Gorgonowa not guilty.

Thirty years later, Horoszewicz shared his sense of the trial with the readers of *Prawo i Życia*: "I got the impression that after discovering the theft, all the shelter residents' automatically suspected the one who had too infamous a name to disappear in the crowd."

We don't know when or why she leaves Warsaw. Could it be because of the humiliation of the trial for stealing a purse?

FOLLOWING LEADS: IN THE ARCHIVES

Until 1941, the files from the trial were located in the District Court in Kraków, but they went missing during the war. The final trail led to Warsaw, where the German authorities brought them when Gorgonowa stood accused of theft. They were sent back to Kraków but never made it to the court. One of the doctors working at the Kraków Forensics Institute intercepted them and hid them from the Germans. I don't know his name, but it's thanks to him that today, in a government archive in Kraków, I can request the full archival documents for criminal case IV 1K 258/32.

The files comprise 1,950 numbered pages in seven volumes. They include photos of the bloodstains on the walls; a woman's work-worn hands with chipped fingernails; smashed windowpanes; the boiler room in the basement near the pool; the room with the exit onto the porch; and the naked corpse of a girl on a large, steel table. Press clippings and an empty envelope marked "Gorgonowa's hair." Letters written by the daughter to her father and her passport with a visa to Switzerland. Thousands of pages of transcriptions of witness testimony in pencil and ink. Typed court transcripts from Kraków and Lwów.

The methods of interrogating witnesses, transcribing the trials, conducting disputes between the defense and the prosecution, do not diverge from modern judicial standards. Something else, though, is surprising: the court's great, meticulous care in investigating the tiniest details and testing the most peculiar hypotheses. Hence the testimony of masses of witnesses completely irrelevant to the case, like Lusia's friends from school, who only remember that she was a nice girl, or the women who lived next door to the Zarembas in Brzuchowice, who once saw Lusia in a summer coat in winter (which supposedly demonstrated Gorgonowa's mistreatment of the children).

We can see the court didn't rush anything. They let the witnesses talk until they were blue in the face. The defendant got that privilege too, telling the court in detail about her life from early childhood to her service at the Zarembas' in Brzuchowice. The files tell us much more about her than newspaper readers of the time knew. They contain her letters, witness testimony from the investigation, the opinion of psychiatric experts.

Brought together, the files are by turns melodrama and psychological thriller—about a country girl lured to a large, wealthy city that speaks a different language, who is thrown out onto the street and left to fight for survival. She manages to hold her own. Things start to go right when she meets a much older, level-headed, caring gentleman who falls hopelessly in love with her. He becomes her life partner. They live relatively happily in a little house near the forest, but in time they grow apart. Then her partner's teenage daughter enters the picture and starts trying to fight off her competitor. Daddy's beloved daughter fuels his aversion to the stranger. And now the father is finally sending his governess-and-lover out of the house. And right when that is meant to happen, Lusia is murdered.

In the run-up to the tragedy, Gorgonowa is like a cornered rat. The fewer ways out she sees, the more aggressive she becomes. With nowhere to retreat to, she'll attack. It's her only chance of survival.

"There was something ominous in the air," said many witnesses in the courtroom. But reading the files doesn't reveal any new evidence.

There's nothing in them that journalists reporting on the trial in the 1930s didn't already write about.

There are hundreds of pages of complex blood analyses and counter-analyses. Expert opinions. Defense motions. And a description of the defense's constant battle to dismiss a string of material evidence, discredit prosecution witnesses, deflect guilt onto Zaremba, and make Rita Gorgonowa out to be a victim.

Mixed in are pages of testimony from those who say she was a cruel and wicked stepmother to the children, and others who say she cared for the children and would never do them harm.

Some say she was promiscuous and vengeful; others, that she had a good heart. Some say she was hard-working; others that she was lazy.

Who speaks with confidence and who jabbers nervously? Who sweats, whose hands shake, whose voice trembles? The records do not say. But without these details it's hard to sense the atmosphere surrounding the trial's participants in the courtroom and to assess which of the witnesses are speaking the truth, and which are lying.

FOLLOWING LEADS: THE NEWSPAPERS

Sixty years after the verdict, the journalist Irena Krzywicka, who reported on the Kraków trial in 1933, still stands by Gorgonowa. "The pressure that played a role in the Gorgonowa case was societal, not political—the pressure of self-righteousness running wild. The presiding judge was conducting the trial in a way that would ensure that the supposed murderess was convicted," she writes in her memoirs, published in 1992.[11] By then, Krzywicka is 93 years old and still convinced Rita was innocent. She suspects Lusia Zarembianka might have been killed by the gardener, Józef Kamiński. "That possibility always seemed to me the most probable," she notes.[12] And she reminds her readers that at the trial in Kraków, Kamiński behaved strangely. He fainted unexpectedly when the judge posed the first question. And when he was carried out of the courtroom, the court completely called off his questioning.

She meant this to be evidence of Kamiński's impure conscience and the partiality of the court. Except it never happened. Kamiński was called into Kraków on March 12, 1933 and gave very precise testimony that was relevant to the case, incriminating Gorgonowa.

---

11 Irena Krzywicka, *Wyznania gorszycielki* [Confessions of a Scandal-Monger], Warsaw: Czytelnik, 1992, p. 290.
12 Ibid., p. 291.

But before he'd even started testifying, Gorgonowa's defense counsel, Maurycy Axer, attacked him, accusing him of murdering Lusia Zarembianka. Kamiński bore these attacks calmly. Krzywicka's memory deceived her. He wasn't the one who fainted that day, it was his exhausted wife Rozalia, who testified in the evening.

But in her articles from 1933 in *Wiadomości Literackie*, Krzywicka doesn't mention the gardener caught up in the murder. Instead she focuses on ticking off lists of police and investigative errors, and also questioning the evidence that implicates Gorgonowa.

"Circumstantial evidence and suspicions are not yet proof of guilt, and Staś's testimony isn't worth a thing," she writes.[13]

In her opinion it was the police who planted the idea of Gorgonowa in young Zaremba's mind, and he believed it and unknowingly repeated it. ("The feeble seedling of his experiences was frozen into the lifeless form of the words he'd prepared and that he would thoughtlessly repeat for the rest of his life.")[14]

Can we believe her?

The thesis about young Zaremba being manipulated is extremely far-fetched and contradicted by the testimony of many other witnesses—for before Staś told the police officers about the woman in the fur coat he saw in the foyer, he shared his discovery with Rozalia and Józef Kamiński. So he couldn't have been manipulated by the police.

Krzywicka says outright that she doesn't believe the defendant is guilty and that there isn't enough evidence to convict her. But the only way to defend Gorgonowa is to destroy the credibility of the main witness—Stanisław Zaremba. So Krzywicka stretches facts, exaggerates testimony that's beneficial to the defendant, and calls into question anything that might harm Gorgonowa: not only that Staś got out of bed quickly, but also whether he could have seen anything

13 Krzywicka, "Wielkie manewry sądowe" [Great Judicial Maneuvers], *Wiadomości Literackie*, May 21, 1933.
14 Ibid.

in the dark, and whether Rita could have run around the house so quickly, smashed the pane in the porch door and gotten into her room, pretending nothing had happened.

But Krzywicka knows, after all, that the whole sequence was timed out, with stopwatch in hand.

From the moment the dog barked, jolting Staś out of sleep, to the moment he went to the glass door and saw the figure moving out into the garden, 22.5 seconds elapsed; he spent 28.6 seconds in Lusia's room and 8.1 seconds went by between running out of his sister's room and hearing the smash of the broken pane in the porch door. Theoretically, Gorgonowa would have had time to get from the front door, where Staś saw her, back to her room. The experts calculated that route along the house, with stops, took 32.5 seconds.

But Krzywicka ignores this.

The German writer Elga Kern also disagrees with the guilty verdict. She writes of a miscarriage of justice. Meanwhile she attempts her own forensic experiment. To prove a person could have easily curbed the Zarembas' formidable dog Lux, she gets her assistant to jump over the fence in Brzuchowice and ply the dog with food. Then she announces that an intruder could have done the same on the night of the killing. Only how was he meant to get across the snow without leaving footprints? How was he meant to sneak into the house? And escape it after the killing? This she doesn't explain.

Elga Kern's article in *Wiadomości Literackie*[15] is a fiery manifesto in defense of Gorgonowa, but it includes no hard evidence of her innocence. Instead, it's a judicial polemic, the opinion of an engaged person making her own judgment on the case, rather than a cold analysis of the facts.

It's hard to agree with Kern when she writes that the Lwów trial was a "long string of claims speaking in Gorgonowa's favor," and that

---

15 Elga Kern, "Prawda o procesie Gorgonowej" [The Truth About the Gorgonowa Trial], *Wiadomości Literackie*, June 19, 1932.

the expert testimony of doctors and chemists "discredited point by point the circumstantial evidence on which the charges were based." In her article, Kern doesn't even attempt to address young Zaremba's testimony incriminating Gorgonowa. She only dismisses it as vague. She views it as completely impossible from a psychological perspective for a woman to commit such an awful crime. And she proposes the fantastical hypothesis that Staś implicated Gorgonowa because he was under the influence of lunar rays.

There's another reason Kern's articles aren't credible sources of information. Simply put, she didn't speak Polish. She only knew a few very basic words. Even her correspondence with the editors of *Wiadomości Literackie* took place in German. She wrote her pieces in German, and they were then translated. It's hard to consider her fully capable of analyzing a trial where, in addition to the witnesses, numerous experts also took the stand, testifying about complicated medical tests, studies of the murder weapon, and searches for a blood type—all in Polish. At best Elga Kern could only learn about their testimony second-hand, through an interpreter.

FOLLOWING LEADS: THE LIGHT AT THE END OF THE TUNNEL

Michał Olechnowicz receives a visit to his office from the owner of a gardening company called Ecoogród. When the potential client asks about clearing someone's name, what comes to mind is overturning convictions from unjust communist show trials. Then she specifies that she's talking about her grandmother, who got into some trouble before the war. The potential client is Margarita, Ewa Ilić's daughter, and when she mentions her grandmother's last name, everything clicks into place. When she asks if he'll take on the case, he doesn't hesitate.

News ricochets around Poland about the then-thirty-five-year-old lawyer from Szczecin who's taking on the legendary case. A long line of journalists forms in front of his office to ask about every detail from eighty years before.

"What makes you wonder the most?" asks *Rzeczpospolita*.

"It's not certain at all that a woman dealt the fatal blows. The ice-axe was heavy, so the killer had to be exceptionally strong. [. . .] We might think the attacker simultaneously held down the girl and delivered blows that caused deep wounds. I doubt a woman would be so strong."

"Do you think you'll manage to remove the brand of murderess from Gorgonowa?"

"We have to try," he replies.

Today we have more knowledge, psychiatry, and psychology are on a higher level—maybe those determinations or analyses contain errors. [. . .] Maybe we'll be able to undermine the expert report on Lusia's brother's perceptive abilities; the renowned lawyers defending Gorgonowa previously tried to question his credibility.

He tells *Wprost*:

The fact that the trial took place 82 years ago is irrelevant. If we manage to find new evidence, that will be grounds for reopening the case. [. . .] I think that years later we have the chance to find evidence that could allow us to clear her name.

And *Gazeta Wyborcza*:

There were already plenty of voices in 1932 and 1933 saying this was not so much a circumstantial trial as charging an innocent person based on cherry-picked facts and interpretations. Today an impartial analysis of the files must lead a reader to conclude that this is exactly what happened.

From the windows of his practice in the center of Szczecin, Michał Olechnowicz can see the tall tower of the detention center where his usual clients wait for him behind bars. The Gorgonowa trial is a completely different animal. A legend and a chance to make a mark on the history of a case that law students dream about. That said, Olechnowicz has heard that several of his more senior colleagues declined because they thought the case was hopeless.

"When a charge goes to trial, every case seems similarly hopeless, but acquittals do happen. It's worth a try," he says.

Still, to reopen the case, he'd have to bend over backward, find new, strong evidence whose existence was unknown to the court in the 1930s. And then he'd have to convince the Supreme Court in Warsaw that Gorgonowa really was innocent. That would open the way to a new trial. But who would testify at such a trial, when all the witnesses to the event, and all the expert witnesses who testified, are now dead? How would a court verify the evidence and the mutually contradictory witness testimony?

Legal authorities tell the media it's impossible.

"On that basis we could go all the way back to medieval trials," says former Justice Minister Zbigniew Ćwiąkalski dismissively, "because you can be sure witches burned at the stake didn't commit a crime."

At first, Olechnowicz was still a moderate optimist. He saw himself running a few forensic experiments, intending to reconstruct the course of events of eight decades before.

"Even if I'd done that," he says today, "then in the opinion of the experts I spoke to, we wouldn't be able to treat it as discovering new evidence unknown to the court, which is required to reopen a trial. And that's a problem, because with the passage of time, certain important pieces of evidence aren't possible to test, while others are decayed beyond repair."

Searching for documents in Ukraine also turned out to be a dead end. (During the Second World War, the Soviets transferred the Lwów archives to Moscow.)

Today he says he has to respect the legally valid verdict convicting Gorgonowa. ("If we look at it objectively, there's more pointing to her guilt than her innocence.") So he's looking for something that can undermine that verdict. That might be one crowning piece of material evidence or a strong combination of circumstantial evidence to break apart the whole of the charges.

Except that for the time being he's found nothing.

"I'm looking for a foothold," he admits.

He definitely won't find it in the slim paper folder of files on the case, which he pulls from a filing cabinet. It contains nothing but letters sent from all over Poland, with ideas of where Gorgonowa might have hidden out after leaving prison.

"Since there's no proof of her innocence, maybe she was guilty?" I ask.

"As a lawyer I can't say that she did it. I won't lay down my weapons. I'm waiting. But it's probably more possible to establish what happened to Gorgonowa after the Second World War than to find that single, new piece of evidence in the case that would allow us to reopen the trial."

FOLLOWING LEADS: THE MOVIE

In 1977, the director Janusz Majewicz returns to the events in his film *The Gorgonowa Case*. The villa in Brzuchowice is represented by the mansion of the Lilpop industrial dynasty in Komorów, outside Warsaw; the Lwów court, by the tsarist-era mess hall in the Modlin Fortress; and the court in Kraków by a courtroom on Leszno Street in Warsaw.

To this day it's one of the best Polish courtroom dramas. Majewski meticulously recreates the trial and the atmosphere surrounding it. His point is not to solve a decades-old murder mystery, but to show the judicial machine, dehumanizing and ruthless.

Gorgonowa, played by Ewa Dałkowska, is sympathetic. She has none of the arrogance and peevishness that made her so disliked in Kraków and Lwów, while she does show noble suffering and uncertainty. Because Majewski is toying with the viewer. Once the audience allows themselves to think that Gorgonowa definitely was the killer, he leads them by the nose and rattles their certainty.

The film keeps us in suspense to the end and doesn't offer an answer to the most important question: who did it?

"Unfortunately, *The Gorgonowa Case* explains nothing," laments *Tygodnik Powszechny* just after the première.

217

CEZARY ŁAZAREWICZ

Despite the tepid review, crowds pack into movie theaters all over Poland. People grow interested again in Gorgonowa, the legends and discussions spring back to life: guilty or not guilty? The whole of Poland is searching for her again. If she's alive, she'd be seventy-six. Not so old. Would she have gone to see herself on the big screen? Would she thank the director for not crucifying her? For discovering the human being in her and putting the audience's sympathies on her side? (Before the war, the newspapers reported that Hollywood intended to bring her story to the silver screen, but lost interest when the District Court in Kraków confirmed the charges and convicted Gorgonowa of murder. Without a happy ending, her story lost its commercial potential.)

Majewski is from Lwów. He first encountered Gorgonowa's story before the Second World War. He was still a child, and when he refused his meals, his nanny threatened him with something worse than a witch: "If you don't eat your porridge, Gorgonowa will come and kill you," she said.

He learned who this awful, wicked woman was after the war, in the late 1940s, when he read about the Brzuchowice killing in old annuals of *Tajny Detektyw*.

"The story stuck in my memory because none of it was ever completely explained," says the eighty-six-year-old director, drinking coffee in a café on Unia Lubelska Square in Warsaw. On May 21, 1976, he read the trial records in the Kraków State Archive and under "purpose of use" he wrote: "work on a film script." He admits that after reading them, he had serious doubts about whether Gorgonowa was really the killer.

He turned to an acquaintance, the theater director Erwin Axer, son of the lawyer Maurycy Axer. Erwin took him to see his mother, Maurycy's widow. Majewski asked her directly: "Did your husband believe she was innocent?"

"He had moments of doubt," replied Ernestyna Axer, "but when he spoke to Mrs. Gorgonowa, his faith returned to him. He defended her with conviction."

"It was a thrilling story, and I wanted to tell it in the language of film," says Majewski today. "I scoured the files, memoirs, and old newspapers to find as many details as possible, to recreate the 1930s and the atmosphere at the time."

He says what permitted him to fulfill his ambitions was the adroit casting of Ewa Dałkowska. She was riveting. The dialogue, which Majewski wrote with the screenwriter Bolesław Michałek, was a mix of fact and fiction; they were not trying to offer a documentary recreation of the trial, but instead to plant the seeds of doubt in viewers' minds.

"I wasn't trying to find an answer to the question: who did it? I wanted the viewers themselves to answer it. I wanted to show the aura around the trial. Could the gardener have done it? I'm not sure. He was never charged, never accused, but certain circumstantial evidence pointed to him. For instance, the ice-axe Zarembianka was killed with. That was a tool of his trade, after all. There were more doubts. We were hoping the film would spark discussion and after the première someone would turn up who'd say: 'yes, it was Gorgonowa,' or 'it wasn't her and it all happened completely differently.'

"No one like that came forward," adds Majewski.

He got a letter from London, from Jerzy Kulczycki, owner of the publishing house Orbis Books. His father, investigative judge Zdzisław Kulczycki, had led the investigation against Gorgonowa in Lwów. When Jerzy was eight years old, Judge Kulczycki was arrested and in 1940 he was shot by the NKVD. In his letter, Jerzy Kulczycki thanked Majewski for casting the renowned actor Andrzej Łapicki as his father. "I still hope to be in Warsaw long enough to meet you and Mr. Łapicki and thank you personally," he wrote.

Richard, the son of Jerzy (who died in 2013) and grandson of Judge Kulczycki, is a computer scientist in London. He replies by e-mail:

"Unfortunately, no family documents have survived, and my grandfather was very discreet. I remember my father once said there was no justification for sentencing Gorgonowa to death. He must have known that from Granddad. But how would he have known about it? Not from Granddad, because the last time he saw him he was eight years old, and Babcia Marysia never talked about it."

JÓZEF K. CAUGHT IN A TRAP

The afternoon of Wednesday, April 20, 1949, Józef Kamiński read in *Express Wieczorny Ilustrowany* that he was dead. It was on the front page in large, bold letters: "DYING GARDENER'S SENSATIONAL TESTIMONY!"

They meant him. The author, Stefania Szatkowska, wrote that preparations were underway in Kraków for the trial of the century because the recently-deceased gardener, Józef Kamiński, had confessed just before his death to murdering Lusia Zarembianka. This was justification for clearing the name of Margarita Gorgonowa, who, in her notorious pre-war trials, had been convicted of murder. (This difficult, challenging, and unprecedented new case is meant to be led by the well-known Kraków lawyer Józef Różański.)

Kamiński read that he'd been wracked by pangs of conscience on his deathbed. This information came from Józef Keller, whom Kamiński didn't know, but who assured *Express* that he was present at the gardener's death. He said of the deceased: "He was an unpleasant man, nervous and gloomy."

Two days later, Kamiński read that he had also confessed to his wife Rozalia about killing Lusia. In the following article, Szatkowska focused on Rozalia, claiming that, after she learned her husband's secret, she wrestled with her emotions until she had a mental breakdown.

Szatkowska's article is reprinted by dozens of Polish newspapers. The news that Kamiński could have murdered Lusia seems very reliable. The sensation travels from mouth to mouth, city to city, village to village. And it spreads like wildfire because it draws on widely shared memories. After all, seventeen years earlier, Gorgonowa's defense lawyer Maurycy Axer had accused Kamiński outright of murdering Zarembianka. ("Since the murder was in a sexual context," he argued at the time, "it could not have been committed by a woman.") He ruled out Staś and Zaremba, leaving him only with Kamiński. And, without any evidence, he cast this terrible suspicion on him.

After that, the pre-war newspapers picked up the subject.

They remind their readers that Kamiński and his wife lived in a separate building. According to testimony, he slept in the kitchen. Before going to bed, he was reading a book. His wife woke him up when she heard knocking on the window and Gorgonowa calling: "Groundskeeper, something terrible's happened!" They thought she meant a radiator had burst from the cold.

A nationwide debate rages in the press about whether the gardener could have killed Lusia. (They printed pictures of him: slim, bald, clean-shaven.) Because of this slander, Kamiński struggles to put food on the table. He has a wife and small child to support, but he can't find work anywhere. Wherever he goes, people say they're scared of him.

"Because of this unjust and harmful smear campaign, my family and I are in extreme poverty," he complains to the Lwów office of *Ilustrowany Kurier Codzienny*. And he threatens to sue: "I want to finally clear my name and I'll sell the shirt off my back to do so, but I'm going to press charges against Gorgonowa's defense team for defamation."

Kamiński doesn't take action until 1950. After consulting with his brother, a priest, he files a complaint with the public prosecutor against Stefania Szatkowska.

A year later the case comes before a court in Kraków. On the defense bench: the author Stefania Szatkowska, editor-in-chief Ryszard Wojna, and their main source, the lawyer Józef Różański. The case is fairly straightforward because Kamiński is alive.

The court finds he has fallen victim to rumors that have long circulated in Poland. These made it all the way to Erwin Gorgon in America, who hired a lawyer in Kraków to find witnesses to Kamiński's death and officially confirm that he was the killer. Różański told Szatkowska about Erwin Gorgon's letter and the rumors going around Poland. He assured the court he had no influence on her publication.

The court awards Kamiński 250,000 złotys in damages and orders an apology to be published in the newspaper.

The apology never appears.

In 1957, Wiesław Naumowski, a reporter for *Po Prostu* magazine, finds Kamiński in Kluczbork. By now the gardener is fifty-six years old. He's bitter. ("He has tears in his eyes," writes Naumowski.)

"It's not about me," Kamiński explains. "I have two grown daughters and a son, I want to leave them a clean name. I don't want them to be branded with this crime. It's awful, but so far no one has helped me recover my reputation. I'm begging you, please clear me of this accusation."

Naumowski can't know at the time that there's no way he can help, either.

In 1968, Kamiński wins another slander case, against *Dziennik Łódzki*. It doesn't change a thing. Kamiński will fight the suspicions to the end of his days. Journalists, historical researchers, and academics will keep citing Szatkowska's article.

In March 1973, Edmund Żurek of *Prawo i Życie* comes to Kluczbork. Kamiński is now an old, troubled man, still battling defamation. He reluctantly talks about Gorgonowa's court cases and his own, with him and his wife fighting for their good name.

"He still lives with the brand of a murderer," writes Żurek after meeting the gardener.

(And to this day nothing has changed. Online you can find 462 pages claiming that Kamiński was the one who killed Lusia.)

FOLLOWING LEADS: LOOKING FOR
A HOOK

He's somewhat younger than Maurycy Axer was when he took on Gorgonowa's defense. And like him, he offers free advice to the poor, the needy, victims of the State. He defended *pro bono* Hubert H., a homeless man charged with insulting then-President Lech Kaczyński. He's also defended a woman who wrote online that an important government minister had blood on her hands. To his mind, she had the right to criticize.

Like Axer, he also takes on hopeless cases. Such as that of Zenon Kwiecień, who was accused of attempting to blow up the Polish parliament. (He persuades the court that Kwiecień is no terrorist, but rather a victim of provocation by the security services.)

He bikes to our meeting, removes his backpack, and takes out some files. He looks like the front man of a punk band who's just come from rehearsal in a garage, not a member of the Kraków Bar. He irritates the legal establishment because he rides to court on that same bike. He walks into the courtroom with his hair messed up and no tie. But he also inspires respect because he defends passionately, is enormously knowledgeable, and speaks with precision.

"My shabby appearance is irrelevant to my clients, who've lost all hope and need a miracle worker," says Maciej Burda, the forty-two-year-old lawyer, in response to his critics.

I've sent him the scanned Gorgonowa files with a request to find what he might be able to seize onto if he were defending Gorgonowa and her life depended on him.

He calls back a few days later. He doesn't have good news. He says the case was run by the book. It was clear from how the evidence was checked and how every possible expert was called, even secondary ones who were meant to explain such marginal phenomena as the groundwater level under the villa in Brzuchowice.

"The court put a solid effort into solving the case and it's hard to find any mistakes here," he says. "This evidentiary material was diligently assessed by the court and points to the conclusion that Gorgonowa was the killer. I respect this verdict, and if I had been one of the judges, I'd have been happy to sign it."

Would he defend Gorgonowa?

"That would be a really interesting job. A closed circle of suspects, limited possibilities of evidence. It's a like mystery out of an Agatha Christie novel. They tried every possible means of solving it, all the evidence was examined, all the experts and witnesses were questioned. They checked everything they could.

"In a situation like this, the only job left for the defense is to interpret and try to impose its own conclusions, to convince the court of its version of events and to undermine the prosecution's version."

What does he think would be his best strategy?

"Similar to Maurycy Axer, I'd question the credibility of the witnesses and the evidence. I wouldn't have another solution."

How would he aim to do it?

"For the defense, the most problematic witness was Staś. You'd have to weaken his credibility and then direct suspicion at him or his father. Zaremba was arrested and initially accused of complicity in the murder, but it would be hard to convince a court that he'd killed his daughter. It would be easier to go after Staś. Nowadays we could commission psychological tests to give us a chance of exploiting that angle."

Does he see a chance of reopening the case?

"Under current procedure, no. Because some new facts or evidence would have to emerge. I don't see that as a possibility."

When asked what he'd do today to solve a similar case, he replies:

"The members of the household would be given polygraph tests, Staś would be questioned in the presence of a psychologist, the experts would have to look more closely at whether the blows could have been struck with an ice-axe. Additional expert opinions would be called in: dactyloscopic, traceological, mechanoscopic, genetic. Every defense lawyer would start with genetics and mapping a DNA profile. It would have been much easier to establish which bloodstains were from Lusia and which from Gorgonowa."

THE LAST WITNESS

There is one more person who witnessed the incidents in the villa the night of December 30–31, 1931: Romusia, the daughter of Rita Gorgonowa and Henryk Zaremba. Only she's not easy to find, because Zaremba, knowing even before the war that people like me would try to track her down, erased every trace of her, concealing his daughter from the world.

"Romusia is my replacement for Lusia. She never loved her mother and never mentions her," Zaremba said of her.[16]

He not only legally changed her name, but also her date of birth from 1928 to 1929, so it wouldn't be so easy to find her by her birth certificate. The last name Zaremba, the final attribute linking her to the tragic story of Brzuchowice, was lost in the 1940s when she got married. She became anonymous.

In the 1970s, after the première of Majewski's film, the judicial reporter Wanda Falkowska found her in Warsaw.

"Before me sits a lady, still very handsome, though not in her first youth. Short-trimmed, salt-and-pepper hair, large, black eyes gaz-

16 "Architekt Zaremba ma dużo do powiedzenia o Gorgonowej – ale po rozprawie" [Architect Zaremba Has Much to Say About Gorgonowa—But After the Trial], *Ilustrowany Kurier Codzienny*, no. 100, April 10, 1933.

ing benignly at the world, a shy smile that contributes to her grace," writes Falkowska about their meeting.

Romusia was forty-nine at the time and it was the first time she'd spoken to journalists about her childhood: Brzuchowice, the loss of her father, her love for Lusia, her fear of her mother. She talks to Falkowska about her impressions of the movie, which she saw the day before.

"Everything seems completely different from how I remember it: the villa in Brzuchowice but also Father and Mother and Lusia. I know there's a lot of imagination in my memories, that they definitely aren't faithful. But I keep going back to my childhood. The case, so far away, so unreal now, keeps weaving in and out of my life like the chorus of a song."

Thirty years later Jakub Kowalski of *Rzeczpospolita* talked her into speaking again. I ask him to put me in touch with Romusia. He tells me I haven't got a prayer.

"Her daughter protects the old woman from those tragic memories," he said.

He suggested I write her a letter. I wrote not that I want to know who killed Lusia, but that I intend to shine a light on her father, Henryk Zaremba, after he was unjustly rumored to be complicit in the crime.

A week later I'm standing in front of a door in an apartment block in Warsaw's Żoliborz district (right next to Dworzec Gdański metro station).

She invites me into a dimly lit room. Now her name is Aldona K.

Her salt-and-pepper hair is now platinum, her black eyes have gone cloudy. That light, shy smile I read about from Falkowska has remained.

She remembers everything.

The front entrance to the house in Brzuchowice was through the main porch to the foyer. On the right was Lusia's room, which her father later turned into an office. Straight on was the living room. That's where they ate. A table and twenty-four carved chairs that her father brought from the mountain resort of Zakopane.

Coming by train from Lwów, you'd approach the house from behind, through a little gate, where the lodge stood. Across from it was the vegetable garden. Over there was the gardener's quarters, the stable, and the garage, where her father kept his Fiat.

The whole house was surrounded by a wall, except on the side facing Marszałkowska Street; there was a picket fence by the main gate. Tour groups coming from Lwów would stand near there and point out to one another the windows of Lusia's room and Gorgonowa's bedroom. The gardener would walk out to them and pour them some water.

She was three-and-a-half at that time. She remembers Lusia, who called her Musia for short. That night there was no electricity in the house, so they ate dinner by candlelight. Then Lusia asked Gorgonowa if she could take Musia to bed with her for the night:

"Who ever heard of such a big girl sleeping with a baby?" protested Rita sharply.

After dinner someone picked her up and put her to bed in her crib. Why she slept in her father's room and not her mother's, she doesn't remember.

It was Staś's unnaturally animal scream that woke her up. She opened her eyes, stood up in her crib and peered into the darkness. Then she heard the low, calm voice of her father, who was leaning over her:

"Daddy's going to go see what's going on and then he'll come right back to Musia."

He disappeared into the darkness and was gone for a very, very long time. Based on the whispers, sobs, footsteps, and creaking coming from the darkness, she tried to guess what was happening on the other side of the wall. And she could sense that something very bad had happened. Fear paralyzed her. She trembled, sobbed, cried out, but no one came to her. Not her father, not her mother, not Lusia. Not until the morning, when it was already light out, did someone's arms open over the crib and carry her out of a house full of strange people. Her mother and father were sitting at the long wooden table in the dining room. She was wearing a brown fur coat, he, a winter jacket. They were strangely distant, unfamiliar, altered.

Romusia was put in a car and driven to Lwów. For five weeks she lived with her father's friends, Mr. and Mrs. Kiszakiewicz.

She didn't know about the blood-soaked bed or the murder. The first time she realized she'd never see Lusia again was at the Bernardine Church, by the silver-colored coffin and amid the vast crowds surrounding it.

She remembers her joy when her father returned from detention after five weeks, and also him falling apart after his firm went bankrupt. He was the one who told her that her mother would never come back to them. She burst into tears. "I don't have a mama anymore," she said. And she quickly forgot about her.

In 1937, her father sold the house in Brzuchowice and they moved to Warsaw. She never went back to Brzuchowice. All she has left from there are seven photos. The rest burned in 1944 in the Warsaw Uprising.

First they lived at 14 Wiejska Street. Then, until the Uprising broke out, in a villa at 24 Rohatyńska Street. In front of the house stood a statue of a flower girl, brought from Brzuchowice, and inside, the chairs from Brzuchowice. The house wasn't as big as the one in the suburbs.

You could get to her father's office through the dining room. Inside he had a large desk. Hanging on the wall was Stanisław Wyspiański's painting *The Resurrection of Lazarus*, also brought from Brzuchowice. (Her father supported artists and made friends with them.)

Once, she went into his office and saw her father seated beneath the painting. He was holding his head in his hands, trembling, and tears were running down his cheeks. It was a Thursday evening, January 5, 1939. Lying on the desk was a telegram from Zakopane, saying Staś had gone missing in the mountains. He was twenty-two years old.

The next day the papers wrote about three skiers from Danzig Technical University who got swept away by an avalanche.

Her father went straight to Zakopane, hoping Staś had survived. But no. Rescue volunteers searched for his body for many months. And only in May, when the snows were melting, did they find it, inside a rock crevice.

FOLLOWING LEADS: ŻUREK

I've walked paths trodden down by his own feet, I've rubbed shoulders with people he met years ago. Back then, he asked them about details, asked for photos, documents, mementoes. And he recorded every conversation on tape. He has a forty-year head start on me. Today, the witnesses to the events are dead . . .

His name is Edmund Żurek—thirty-five-years old then, eighty-six today, a judicial correspondent for the publication *Prawo i Życie*, author of collections of reportage and the most important book of all for him: *Gorgonowa and Others*.

At the time, the editor-in-chief of the low-circulating *Prawo i Życie* had announced a contest among journalists for an article to increase the newspaper's sales. Żurek proposes a series on the most notorious pre-war criminal trial.

How does he know it will take off?

From author events. He tells his readers the behind-the-scenes stories of the most famous trials of recent years (the Warsaw professor Kazimierz Tarwid, accused of poisoning his wife; the Kraków driving instructor Władysław Mazurkiewicz, who shot his victims in the back of the head; the farmer Józef Zakrzewski and two of his sons from the village of Rzepin, who didn't like Mayor Lipa's family and so murdered all five of them one night with axes), but in the end everyone only asks about a trial from forty years ago.

With Gorgonowa's trial, people remember the names of the defense lawyers, the witnesses, they know the evidence, hard and circumstantial, the court proceedings and the private life of the defendant and her family.

They want to know if Gorgonowa really did it.

"I'll take responsibility for the Gorgonowa case myself," Żurek says. "I've got the feeling it'll be a bestseller because the case is still alive. Teachers, engineers, seamstresses, and porters still ask me about her."

He was the first journalist to read, page by page, the files of case IV 1K 258/32. That was on March 8, 1972. I know because he signed next to that date on the check-out card. For six weeks he studied the files in the reading room of the Ministry of Justice on Ujazdowskie Avenue in Warsaw. This became a five-part series of articles on the Gorgonowa case published in *Prawo i Życie* from April to mid-May, 1973. Always on the last page of the paper, always a full column.

In his articles he faithfully describes the trial, but he makes no comments and draws no conclusions. He doesn't settle anything, but he points out all the shortcomings of the evidence.

He gives his attention to the hard life of Rita Gorgonowa, whom he writes about with sympathy. He also defends groundskeeper Kamiński against the absurd accusations of murder.

Żurek dedicated his life to the Gorgonowa case. First he tracked down the files, then Ewa "Kropelka" Ilić, then later Józef Kamiński and his wife Rozalia. There were still eyewitnesses alive to tell him their stories. He possesses enormous expertise; he is acquainted with a vast number of documents and the most minute details.

"A beautiful woman was accused of murder, and her victim was a seventeen-year-old who'd been brutally killed, a girl scout, daughter of a famous architect, who was shamefully deflowered after her death," he says. "The case will move people's hearts until the end of time."

Żurek made friends with the Kamińskis and visited them whenever he was in the area of Kluczbork. He'd join them for a meal, join them for tea, and they would tell him about their lives. Once about how when they first came to Kluczbork after the war, they had needed to guard the only horse in the county to make sure no one ate it. And another time, about the night when Lusia was killed. What the Lady said, what she looked like, how she behaved. And how she kept her hands inside her coat.

"I saw blood on Gorgonowa's hands," Kamiński once told Żurek.

"And I believe him," the reporter says today.

In the 1970s, one active participant in Gorgonowa's 1933 Kraków trial was still alive. That was Prosecutor Bogdan Szypuła, who used the files to dispel, step by step, all of Żurek's misgivings.

Szypuła kept telling him: "I don't have the shadow of a doubt."

Edmund Żurek no longer does either. He visits Ewa Ilić in Trzebiatów every chance he gets. Out of sympathy, not journalistic duty. Each time they go for a walk around town, have lunch together, and talk. Ewa tells him she doesn't believe her mother was guilty, but she never asks what he thinks. If she did, he would always be prepared to respond honestly and simply to that most important question for her: "I think it was Rita Gorgonowa who killed Lusia Zarembianka."

"I know saying that would offend Pani Ewa, her daughter and her granddaughter, but I don't have another explanation."

WHERE IS GORGONOWA?

Looking for her is like groping in the dark. I check rumors, speculations, posts on internet forums. In old books, newspapers, township
and county websites.

I read in *Dominik Turobiński*, a parish newspaper, that she lived
in Turobin during the war, in the Roztocze hills, near today's Pol-
ish-Ukrainian border. At the time Turobin was a town; now it's a
village, but the local government is housed in the same building as
before. They should have residential records there. Everyone who
lived for a significant time in Turobin ought to be recorded there.

The municipal building stands on a small green in the middle of
the village, and the residential records are on the ground floor in a
wooden cabinet in the Office of Vital Statistics. They're divided into
volumes. The thickest is from 1943, when terror began in the big
cities. For people fleeing Lublin, Warsaw and Łódź, Turobin became
a safe refuge. Everyone who arrived at that time should have been
registered. The German occupation authorities required it.

A clerk calligraphed the name, date of arrival, and current address
of every new inhabitant in fountain pen on ledger-sized paper. The
Head of the Office of Vital Statistics, Małgorzata Cieśla, now leafs
through hundreds of names, but there's no trace of Gorgonowa.

Professor Roman Tokarczyk of Maria Curie-Skłodowska University, a native of Turobin, finds nothing unusual in that. "She was keeping her head down out of fear for her safety," he says in an e-mail and assures me she really was there. He came across stories about her while writing a monograph on Turobin. Before that, his father had told him about her staying in the town.

He writes that she made money as a trader. She went around the villages in the area purchasing low-grade meat and selling it for a large profit in Lublin. She rented a room near the old post office on Szczebrzeszyńska Street, in the home of Piotr and Albina Puchala. During the war, they ran a tavern there called Piotr's. He claims that although the Puchalas knew Gorgonowa's secret, they were friendly toward her. Unfortunately both the building and the Puchalas are gone now. The family left with their two children, Zosia and Zbyszek, right after the war.

The village pharmacist, councilor, and local historian Adam Romański helps me look for their son. He spoke to him not long ago—now he lives in Szczecin.

A concrete apartment building on the outskirts of the city. Zbyszek rarely leaves the house, because both of his legs have been amputated. He sits by the window in a deep armchair and clicks through the channels on TV.

"Tall, elegant, dark-haired"—that's how he remembers her.

She rented a room in their house on the ground floor. Living next to her was Władek Szewczuk, a Volksdeutscher who was assassinated by Polish partisans. They broke into the Puchalas' tavern and shot him. He died on the floor, lying in a pool of blood. Gorgonowa stood over him, shook her finger at him and said: "I told you you'd end up like this, you bastard."

Then the assassinated Volksdeutscher's room was taken over by an older, elegant gentleman (Puchala doesn't remember his name). In the village they called him "the professor." And this professor fell in love with Gorgonowa (Zbyszek doesn't know what years this happened). The wedding took place in a church in Gródki, and the reception was at the Puchalas' tavern. Zbyszek's father took them to the church in a sleigh.

There should be evidence of this in the parish records.

There's only one church in Gródki, St. Isadore's—a parish of the breakaway Polish-Catholic Church.

The pastor, Henryk Mielcarz, lives with his family in a villa by the small, redbrick church.

He's heard many times about Gorgonowa's wedding, but he's never found any confirmation of it in the documents. He brings an old parish ledger to show that there's no record of Gorgonowa during the war.

"That still doesn't mean anything," he says: the pastors didn't document everything. Nothing can be ruled out. Not even Greek-Catholic Gorgonowa converting just before her marriage. "Because our national church is very tolerant," he adds with a smile.

Gorgonowa leaves Turobin for liberated Lublin in 1944. Alone, because according to Zbyszek Puchala's memory, the professor was no longer with her. He'd died or gone off somewhere. After that, Zbyszek's mother, Albina, only saw her once. They ran into one another on the street in Lublin.

Thirty-four years later, Alojzy Leszek Gzella described her stay in Lublin for *Kurier Lubelski*. In the 1970s he got a visit from Maria Nizioł, who in the spring of 1943 met Gorgonowa in Krasnystaw. By then she was using the first name Emilia and the surname of her late husband—Kańska. Both women met again in August 1945 on Litewski Square in Lublin.

"Rita was perfectly dressed, she looked interesting, she carried herself elegantly. She almost threw her arms around my neck, like a best friend," Nizioł told Gzella.

Kańska invited her friend to her apartment. It was a studio in a small building at 3 Kołłątaj Street, in the very center of the city, on the fourth floor, windows facing the street.

The room was beautifully furnished, and a handsome officer was hanging around in it. Kańska told Maria Nizioł that since she was looking for an apartment she could move in there, because Kańska herself was just leaving for Oleśnica, near Wrocław. She wanted to start her life over, in the "Recovered Lands" Poland was gaining from Germany after the war.

Maria Nizioł brought to the *Kurier Lubelski* office a ration document for 3 Kołłątaj Street, apartment 10, in the name of Kańska. On the back Gorgonowa had written in blue ink that she agreed to accept the Niziołs as subletters.

"I had no right to doubt her," says Gzella today. To him this was an isolated incident. He never looked for Gorgonowa again.

Two weeks after his article was published, a letter came to the *Kurier* from Turobin. In it, a certain Pan Sławek talked about the wartime fate of Rita Gorgonowa's husband. He said "the professor" had gotten arrested for illegal financial operations. He was sentenced to three years in prison. He did his time in Krasnystaw. Gorgonowa apparently visited him regularly. Then he was transferred to another prison and he wasn't heard from again.

"My husband gave me a soul, a great treasure," she once told Sławek on a cart ride from Turobin to Lublin. "He made me happy. He gave me a new name, and to me that was the most important thing—that I'm not called Gorgonowa anymore."

The three-story, freshly painted apartment building at 3 Kołłątaj Street shares one wall with the former Lublin Industrialists' Fund, which before the war held the popular Central Bar.

If she lived here back then, she must have passed soldiers on the street. There was a housing shortage in the bombed city, so the military was stationed in a former monastery, which after the war held the Medical Academy and which today is a cultural center.

The stable-courtyard now holds a pharmacy, a bar called Ramzes, law practices, and the office of a member of the European Parliament, Lena Kolarska-Bobińska. I walk across the paving stones—not the same ones as from back then—to a staircase inside, on the left. No one answers the intercom at number 10. I climb all the way up the old, wooden, creaky stairs to the fourth floor. The hallway is lined with metal doors with no handles or numbers. One of them leads to apartment 10. No one answers when I knock. (These have been unoccupied for a long time, because the floor is covered in a thick layer of dust.) The same one floor down.

Only at number 7 does a young man open the door. He says he's never heard of Gorgonowa.

She's neither in the Lublin population register nor in the Lublin city government archive office.

"Regarding your question I can report we have found no information on Rita Gorgonowa (Emilia Kańska)," replies Dorota Pedrycz Guzek, writing from the Lublin Population Register Office.

The apartment on Kołłątaj Street in Lublin is the last lead. Beyond that, there are only rumors, allegations, suppositions, confabulations, myths, phantasmagorias. Nothing that you can grasp, that you can check, that will carry you one more step. Did she finally reach Oleśnica? Did she live in Wrocław, in Nysa, in Polanica, in Kłodzko? All these names appear in various press publications.

Did she run a clothing store in Olsztyn? Did her windows get smashed there? Did she emigrate to Romania, Yugoslavia, the United States, South America? These places come up in the rumors that circulate to this day.

The journalist Edmund Żurek has been searching for her for four decades longer than I have. For years he's combed through communities of former Lwów residents all across Poland. He's asked about

DID THIS HAND KILL?

her in Bytom, Opole, Wrocław, Szczecin, Zielona Góra. He's asked for help from Yugoslav journalists and the Polish Red Cross. He's visited places where any sort of rumors of her have appeared. And nothing.

"She wasn't anywhere," he says. The trail also went cold for him in Lublin in August of 1945; later, vague leads took him to somewhere in Lower Silesia, where, in the area of Wrocław, he hit a dead end.

He has his theories.

"She went missing in the Recovered Lands right after the upheaval of the war," he says.

FOLLOWING LEADS: THE DNA

The tabloids call him the genetic detective: he can tell from a drop of blood whether it belongs to a human or an animal, to a woman or a man, a perpetrator or a victim.

Professor Ryszard Pawłowski from the Forensics Institute in Gdańsk is the most famous DNA-testing expert in Poland. Seventeen years ago he helped the police in Szczecin identify a serial rapist and murderer prowling Świnoujście. But will he be able to tell Lusia Zarembianka's blood from Rita Gorgonowa's, eight decades later?

"If we have a surviving blood spot a few millimeters square, there's a chance of finding DNA. And we could determine who the blood belonged to," he says and explains over the phone how forensic procedures work since the introduction of DNA testing. Today, these would allow us to easily determine whose blood was found on Gorgonowa's fur coat. If it was Lusia's, that would have been key evidence against Gorgonowa. Was she in contact with the corpse? Then she was the killer.

If evidence with blood on it still exists somewhere, Professor Pawłowski is prepared to test it. And it doesn't matter how long ago it was collected—the important thing is whether it was properly stored.

The material evidence was sent from Lwów on October 11, 1932, and arrived in Kraków in three packages. The court records show it included the fur coat with traces of blood, Lusia's blood-stained nightgown, the feces found in Lusia's room (packed in a metal box), pieces of plaster, and the ice-axe, wrapped in paper. Everything was deposited in the Kraków District Court's material evidence storage facility at location 739/32. In November 1932, the evidence was transferred to the Forensics Institute of the Jagiellonian University's Collegium Medicum at 16 Grzegórzecka Street. Theoretically it could be there to this day.

"Is the material evidence from the Gorgonowa case still located at your facility?" I ask in an e-mail to Professor Tomasz Konopka, the current director of the Kraków institute.

"The only piece of evidence we've retained is the ice-axe with which the murder was committed," he replies.

The Kraków Forensics Medicine Department was founded in 1804 (twenty-one years before one was created in Warsaw). It's one of the oldest in Europe, as you can tell from the building on Grzegórzecka Street. It looks like a museum—arches, columns, stone floors, and portraits of ancestors on the walls. The most important of these is an oil painting of Jan Olbrycht, who laid the foundation of modern forensic medicine. He was the first in Poland to make use of blood in forensic investigations. At the moment there's a pause for a few days in exhuming the victims of the Smolensk air disaster of 2010, so Professor Tomasz Konopka leads me around the institute's memorial room. Glass cases hold the most interesting items, sent here by prosecutors and judges from all over Poland because Kraków was once considered the epicenter of forensic analysis. There are axes, knives, cleavers, hammers, handles—in other words, everything Poles have used over the last century to kill one another.

The two-kilo, handle-less ice-axe looks just like it did in the photograph eighty-five years ago in *Tajny Detektyw*. It's covered with the same rust-brown patina. We can pull it out of the cabinet, examine it, even take it in hand, feign a couple of blows—and feel like the murderer on that night.

"You only need one cell to find DNA, but there are none on this," the professor assures me, turning the ice-axe over in his hands. And even if there once were, over those eighty-five years the ice-axe has gone through thousands of hands—of policemen, prosecutors, judges, lawyers, experts, and even ordinary students who, during their classes, wanted to take a closer look at the most famous of the exhibition items.

Before it ended up in the display case, the ice-axe spent ten hours at the bottom of the pool in Brzuchowice. If there were any traces of blood on it, the water washed them away. When it reached Kraków ten months later, it was covered in a thick layer of brown-red rust. In Kraków, Professor Olbrycht made heavy use of it. First he searched it for blood, and when he found none, moved on to further experiments. He tested cadavers. He was especially interested in their heads. He smashed them with the axe and compared the wounds with those Zarembianka had. He thereby established that the perpetrator was right-handed and struck the girl's head with the dull edge.

Then he used the ice-axe for more experiments. For many weeks, he smeared it in human blood and submerged it in water. He was checking whether the pool could really wash it clean.

For the answer as to who the killer was, Tomasz Konopka suggests looking at Professor Olbrycht's scientific publications.

FOLLOWING LEADS: FROM
OLBRYCHT'S ARCHIVE

In Janusz Majewski's movie, Wojciech Pszoniak played the role of Jan Olbrycht. He portrayed him as a slightly kooky, extremely fanatical scientist cut off from reality—an expert witness who held in his hands the fate of a lost, hounded woman, played by Ewa Dałkowska. He was pretending to be a cool-headed professional, but really he dreamed of destroying Gorgonowa. Pszoniak's Olbrycht is manic, moody, and talks to himself.

This cinematic portrait of a universally respected Kraków professor, who in reality was a model of diligence and impartiality, departed so far from the truth that the late professor's relatives sued Majewski. They demanded an immediate halt to screenings of the film. The court dismissed their case on the basis that Olbrycht's name is not mentioned even once in the movie.

That's true: it isn't. But still, everyone in Kraków knew that the nutty Pszoniak was playing Poland's most famous forensic scientist, whose work laid the foundation of Polish forensic medicine, whose textbooks are still used by medical students.

He joined the Kraków Forensics Institute before World War I. By the twenties, he was renowned as an outstanding authority. He collected experiments, walking around with police officers as they examined crime scenes. He was a pioneer in using serology for forensic investigations.

In 1923, at the age of thirty-seven, he was made director of the Faculty of Forensic Medicine in Kraków, which had been founded especially for him. Three years later he would become the first forensic scientist in Polish courts to use blood-type testing to establish disputed paternity.

He was hailed as a miracle-worker in 1927 when he was able to determine, from hunks of flesh fished out of Dłubnia Creek, that the victim was a young woman killed by blows to the head with a heavy instrument before her body was dismembered. He based these conclusions on fat embolisms in the lungs that occurred after the bones were crushed. (The deceased's head was never found.)

Olbrycht determined not only the cause of death and the perpetrator's actions, but even what the victim looked like. Based on bone measurements, he claimed that the victim was a twenty-eight-year-old woman, 150–160 centimeters in height. He even cast her as a brunette, determining the color based on pubic hair. This fit the description of Zofia Paluch, a Kraków artists' model who had gone missing. The mystery was solved when the police showed up at her husband's apartment and found bloodstains. Olbrycht's analysis incriminated Maciej Paluch, and although he didn't confess, the court convicted him of murdering his wife. Only after a few years in prison did he express remorse and describe how he'd committed the murder. His testimony matched what Olbrycht had previously established.

The professor's home university describes him as: "no-nonsense, brave, objective, diligent, demanding, strict, not remotely an opportunist."

He has several thousand judicial forensic expert reports under his belt, hundreds of criminal mysteries solved, dozens of scientific publications translated into various languages. He appears as an expert witness in very high-profile Nazi war crimes tribunal: of Ludwig Fischer, the governor of the Warsaw district of the General Government; of Josef Bühler, a cabinet minister in the General Government; and of personnel at Auschwitz. But he achieves immortality as the expert witness who incriminated Margarita Gorgonowa. And for his whole professional life, he grappled with this case and the lies about Gorgonowa's innocence.

In the late 1930s, in the face of intensifying rumors, he sets out to meticulously and scientifically dispense with the skeptics. He will do so in an academic article in which he analyzes the files in detail and dispels all doubts.

His work is interrupted by the war. The professor is sent to a concentration camp. First to Auschwitz, then to Mauthausen. He returns to Kraków in 1945. He gets his old scientific team back together and rebuilds the department. Under his leadership, the Institute of Forensic Medicine becomes the most important organization of its type in Poland.

At this time, Olbrycht is training a new army of forensic scientists, writing textbooks for them, and devoting himself zealously to his work.

Does he recall about a certain trial from years ago?

He recalled: "It seemed to me that the Gorgonowa case now belonged to history, that collective interest was likely long past and minds had calmed."

So it remained until 1949. Then *Echo Krakowa* reprints Stefania Szatkowska's notorious article about the gardener, said to confess on his deathbed to the murder of Lusia Zarembianka. All the emotions spring back to life. The memories have returned. All over Poland, Gorgonowa's name is once again on everyone's lips. And now it isn't only the tabloids who are unsure of her guilt, but scientific publications as well.

In *Problemy Kryminalistyki*, Mieczysław Czubalski raises doubts about Gorgonowa's guilt. It's 1960. This is when Olbrycht decides to finish his paper on the subject.

His justification:

> No criminal trial in Poland in recent decades has so violently set the minds of a wide swath of society whirring. We might call it a collective psychosis.
>
> Toward the people called on to try the case, various publications have made expressions of—on the one hand—utmost respect and—on the other—appalling offense. They have held orgies: of dilettantism, malice, and ignorance. Can you imagine how painful it has been for people of expertise and who are informed about the case to read these sorts of demagogical, amateurish assertions? There remains rooted in society an opinion of a miscarriage of justice whose supposed victim is Gorgonowa. Therefore the time has come, after the commentary, for science to have its say as well.

Science—in the pen of Jan Olbrycht—has its say in the book *Selected Cases from Forensic-Medical Practice*. After the professor's death in 1968, his family deposited the manuscript in the Jagiellonian University Library. It is there to this day, in Olbrycht's archive. You need only fill out a request and the archivist will bring the papers to you with white gloves. Sixteen folders. That is how much he left behind.

There are photographs of him. A hunched old man behind a large desk with two ebonite telephones, a stack of papers and a family photo. In other pictures: always in a white lab coat, always with a white shirt and a tie showing underneath it.

DID THIS HAND KILL?

He never smiles; he doesn't look into the camera. In these photos he doesn't look kind, but rather intimidating and off-putting. Cold, high-minded, reserved.

Journalists don't like people like him because they never help out a reporter, never advise, never point the way. Maybe that's why they wrote about him with ill will and suspicion. And in *Wiadomości Literackie*, they say outright that he's biased, hostile to Gorgonowa, and untrustworthy. Such clippings aren't to be found in the professor's archive. There are ones where journalists write about his remarkable achievements, his string of successes, the mysterious deaths he solved. The professor was a man of few words, so there are no interviews with him. Everything he wanted to convey he published in his academic articles. He devoted an entire chapter to Gorgonowa (136 typed manuscript pages) in *Selected Cases from Forensic-Medical Practice*. He's the first forensic scientist to meticulously recreate the last moments of Elżbieta Zarembianka's life.

From the bloody exclamation points and necks of retorts (as he calls the marks on the wall), the position of the body, the size and depth of the wounds, Olbrycht deciphers the direction of the blows, the type of instrument used, and even in which direction the perpetrator fled.

Olbrycht writes that the first blows struck Zarembianka when she was asleep. She lay on her right side, face turned toward the wall. (The blood flowed toward the right side of her body.) The blow was so strong that the ice-axe (the professor does not rule out the possibility of an ice-axe) got lodged in her skull. And she stopped moving.

The following blows were weaker. As if the killer didn't have the strength, as if they were exhausted by the beating. They might have even put the ice-axe aside for a moment to rest.

Beyond that, there are only suppositions: that the girl might have regained consciousness for a moment. The professor knows of such instances from his own practice and descriptions of the case of "The

Vampire of Düsseldorf" (Peter Kürten, who killed women with a hammer).

And Lusia regaining consciousness might have frightened the killer, who grabbed the ice-axe and finished her off. These subsequent blows struck the right side of her head and her arm. (This is evidence that Zarembianka turned her head and instinctively covered her face.)

The cause of Zarembianka's death was brain damage. As she was dying, the falsified rape took place. Falsified because, as the professor demonstrates, the killer broke the girl's hymen with a finger. (He confirms that it was a finger in an experiment on the cadavers of two young women.) "The Gorgonowa case is a contribution to the case history, very sparse in the world of specialist writings, of instances of a falsified lust killing," writes Olbrycht. The professor maintains a scientific distance and tries not to say directly that Gorgonowa was the murderer. But he does not rule out that a woman committed the killing. So he notes that a woman was capable of breaking Zarembianka's hymen and wielding the ice-axe.

And if anyone had further doubts, he specifies that Gorgonowa had enough time to kill Lusia and return to her own room, that she was strong enough and psychologically capable of it.

In his book, Olbrycht dispels one more doubt—the matter of the feces found just after the killing. To the prosecution this was evidence incriminating Gorgonowa because it was meant to prove the murderer was a novice and her nerves gave out. For the defense—on the contrary—it was proof of her innocence, with Axer making the case that only professional burglars leave such a trace of themselves behind. The dispute remained unresolved until Olbrycht became the first scientist to test the recovered samples and determined that they were very likely dog feces.

At the end of the chapter on Gorgonowa, he writes something along the lines of a life motto:

"It is the right and duty of an expert witness to seek the truth above all and to serve truth, regardless of the criticism and hostility of those who dislike objectivity and impartiality."

"The case was based on circumstantial evidence. It was decided by oral statements. And those weighed against Gorgonowa," the director of the Kraków institute Tomasz Konopka tells me today. "Professor Olbrycht's analysis shows the evidence incriminates Gorgonowa. And I agree with him. All of us here have a very high opinion of the professor."

"And you don't have any doubts?"

"I have no reason to doubt. If you look for inconsistencies, you can question any verdict. I myself would be able to find arguments that would impress newspaper readers. You can convince them, but not a court. It's not as if you can read the files carefully and find something there that they overlooked at the time. This case was investigated very carefully. To this day I find documents in our laboratory from experiments on cadavers that the professor performed back then. He was very meticulous. If he says Gorgonowa was the murderer, then she was."

THE SECRETS OF ALDONA K.

In 1940 or 1941, Romusia doesn't remember when exactly, her father married Henryka Jurasz, who had previously been his cousin's wife.

She wanted to call her "Mama," but Henryka only let her go as far as "Auntie." Today she calls her "my stepmother." Her stepmother never let her forget she was the offspring of a criminal and that there was no difference between her and her mother. Romusia didn't like her stepmother, who did everything to make her father hate her, she says, and transfer all his love to his new wife's son, Januszek. The boy was the apple of his eye, while Romusia was just Gorgonowa's daughter.

Changing her name to Aldona—Donia for short—doesn't help much. The kids at school find out her secret. They point fingers at her. She feels like she's worse than them. Under her changed name she still wears the brand of Gorgonowa, which makes her life that much harder. When she's a teenager, she meets Zbyszek. She wants to go dancing with him, but the boy's uncle, a doctor, finds out about it and immediately warns him: "If you get married to Donia, she'll murder your children." Everything falls apart.

Zaremba's new family doesn't have it easy either. People insult the stepmother on the street, shouting after her: "Gorgonowa!" They throw stones at Zaremba. None of this bothers K., a future engineer, and he asks Romusia to marry him.

The K. family live with their daughter in Muranów district in Warsaw, in a single shabby room. He's finishing college; she's supporting the family with her job at the Meatpacking Union, where once a week they pay a share of the workers' wages in kiełbasa.

In 1957, Romusia decides to track down her only sister. Through a journalist who authored an article about Ewa, she learns where she is and brings her to Warsaw. They live together in the single room.

Romusia thinks Ewa isn't hard-working enough, that she should help out more often. Conflict builds, so Ewa finally moves out, breaks off contact, leaves for Pomerania. They don't speak to one another.

Years later, Romusia wants to rebuild her family. During a trip to the shore she decides to visit her sister in the countryside. She goes all the way to Trzebiatów and sees her walking through the town, carrying brushwood she's gathered in the forest. Disheveled, in a tattered dress and shoes that are too big.

The sight terrifies Romusia. She leaves.

Until this moment she hasn't thought about her sister—or her mother, either.

"I lived convinced that she was gone," she says. "My father never mentioned her, so I forgot about her. I didn't think about her. I didn't miss her. Only my stepmother would mention her. She said the most horrible things about her. Afterward I couldn't get close to her, after what she'd done, after seeing how my father suffered. Every year on the anniversary of Lusia's death, he'd lock himself in his office, and you had to walk around on tiptoe. My father was afraid that once my mother got out of prison, she'd start looking for me, and if she found me, she'd want to get closer, pull me over to her side, and take me away from him.

"He was right—she did turn up. By some miracle she found out we lived in Kolonia Kościuszkowska in Żoliborz district. Our house stood between the Chemistry Institute and a Resurrectionist convent. In the foyer there was a large window looking out onto the courtyard. I saw her through it. She was standing in front of the gate in a red coat. I knew right away it was her: she was beautiful, she had black, curly hair. I thought such an elegant woman couldn't be anyone other than Gorgonowa. I got frightened. I ran to the kitchen, where my stepmother was cooking lunch.

"'Auntie,' I said, 'Gorgonowa's come for me.'

"My stepmother went to open the door for her. I heard my mother saying she wanted to see me, and then my stepmother led her to my father's office. My mother sat down in one of those large, leather chairs, but I kept standing on the stairs. I was afraid to go up to her. When she saw me, she started to smile.

"'Child, I'm your mother,' she said in a friendly tone.

"I responded harshly: 'I don't have a mother. And I never did.'

"The smile vanished from her face. She quickly got to her feet and left. Yet she didn't completely erase herself from my life. I used to see her red coat circling near me; I'd always run away from it. When I say the word 'mother,' I don't feel anything. I've never missed her. Her name sickens me. It reminds me of the gorgons, mythical sea monsters. My father never told me what happened in Brzuchowice. I've worked everything out on my own. I overheard my father talking to my stepmother, I've asked people I know, I've read newspapers. I've analyzed the facts and there's no other explanation. She did it.

"It was her bloody handkerchief they found in the basement under the coal. Her prints from the women's slippers in the snow leading to the porch. It was her Staś saw after he woke up.

"And there's another thing that incriminates her, and which Staś only told me much later. That night, as he walked past her bed before he went to sleep, he saw she was holding her book upside down. Clearly she was so nervous she didn't notice. Maybe in her thoughts she was already in Lusia's room?"

THE FINAL LEAD

Margarita Ilić, Rita's granddaughter who lives in Szczecin, passes me one more lead to check out: the village of M., located between Wrocław and Kluczbork.

Recently, a woman wrote to her from there:

> Your grandmother came here, supposedly, when the Germans were still here. She ran a store in the village and lived alone in a large house. The house had a gorgeous garden, oriental plants. There were some little statues in the trees. All that's left is one tree off the road. I checked. It's a tamarisk.
>
> She made friends with some couple, and more or less only with them. Apparently when she disappeared, the police searched for her for a few days. They didn't find anything. The couple said your grandmother left in the night. Shortly afterward the couple took over her house. Their children and grandchildren live there to this day. I suggest searching there.

I follow the lead. It's a five-hour drive from Warsaw on narrow, winding country roads. Along the main road there are ex-German farms with large brick barns, interspersed with small modern houses with plastic windows. The woman behind the counter in the former government store tells me I haven't come in vain and sends me to Babcia Irena.

"She's the oldest. She's nearer the end than not, so maybe she'll tell the truth."

Irena P. arrived in M. in early 1946. She moved into a place on the edge of the forest, because all the houses in the center of town were taken. Her family shared their home with the former German owners, who no longer had the right to the house or the land. When a tree the Germans had planted started dropping pears, they couldn't eat them without asking. They had to get permission from the new owners. Irena's parents weren't vindictive, and they agreed to let the Germans gather fruit for themselves. One day, soldiers and police drove in and ordered all of the Germans out of M. They loaded their possessions onto carts and set off on the main road through the village, where locals pushed the carts into ditches and took from them what they wanted.

Irena says by the time she moved here, Gorgonowa was gone. But her legend, and people who remembered her, remained. They told Irena she lived in Wilejka. Today there's a cemetery not far from where her house was. She only made friends with one couple, the Krzysiaks, who had taken over a German house in the center of the village. And one night she disappeared. When her neighbors asked Krzysiak about her, he replied she was not only a murderer, but also a thief. He claimed she'd stolen a bucket filled with gold and fled. She never came back, no one ever ran into her, no one heard anything about her, and she didn't send anyone a letter or postcard.

"Krzysiak himself would know the most," says the old woman, but quickly remembers he's long dead, after all.

For twenty years, Stanisław Krzysiak has lain in a grave in the little village cemetery, near what used to be called Wilejka, where Gorgonowa lived. Now the Krzysiaks have a new house there, on a property they took over after Gorgonowa disappeared. Stanisław's daughter, Barbara, lives there with her husband. Barbara was born in 1945. Potentially, she may remember Gorgonowa from her parents or neighbors. But when she learns what I want to ask her about, she claims she has a headache. The older gentleman makes a surprised face:

"Do they really say she lived here? First I've heard of it."

So I prompt him with what I've just learned: that she came here in August 1945, that she disappeared in December 1945 or early January 1946. For those four or five months she lived right here, where the Krzysiaks' house now stands. She disappeared one night with his in-laws' gold. And shortly after she disappeared, those in-laws took over her house, as if they knew the owner would never return.

There's no way he hasn't heard this story, since I found out about it the moment I arrived in M.

The older man shakes his head and calmly repeats:

"First I've heard of it."

And he doesn't even bat an eye. He doesn't say another word.

The answer to the mystery comes by e-mail.

"For the people in the village it's no secret what happened there," writes a woman I met earlier in M., but who claimed then that she didn't want to pass on gossip. Now she's changed her mind. "Apparently Gorgonowa was rich. And she had a lot of gold. And when she disappeared, suddenly Mr. and Mrs. Krzysiak took over her house. Supposedly, afterward, Krysiak never went upstairs, into the attic. Some people say they took her corpse into the woods on a cart; others, that it was probably buried in the garden. I'm inclined to believe the second option: the road to the forest would be too risky."

She closes her e-mail with a request: "I'm writing to you in secret. I live here alone with a herd of cattle and a barn that would burn easily. Please understand why I'm afraid."

ACKNOWLEDGEMENTS

Thank you to Jakub Kowalski, who helped me contact Romana Zarembianka, the daughter of Henryk and Rita. Without him I could not have reached the final living witness of the crime in Brzuchowice. And to Magda Kicińska, who searched for post-war traces of Rita Gorgonowa in Lublin.

To Małgorzata Weiss, the director of the Koszalin Public Library's Audiovisual Collection Division, for keeping on the archival alert for the sake of my book.

I would like to especially thank Irena Pokazanova from Lviv, whose blog and advice I used when wandering through Lviv and Briukhovychi in search of traces of Rita Gorgonowa and Henryk Zaremba.

And Ewa, for her support and being a point of reference. There's no one else I can share my doubts with as I work.

BIBLIOGRAPHY

Books:

Axer, Erwin, *Ćwiczenia pamięci*, Warsaw: Państwowy Instytut Wydawniczy, 1991

Ibid., *Z pamięci*, Warsaw: Wydawnictwo "Iskry," 2006

Falkowska, Wanda, "Gorgonowa—sprawa bez końca," *Express Reporterów* 1978 no. 2, Krajowa Agencja Wydawnicza, Warsaw

Hirszfeld, Ludwik, *Historia jednego życia*, Kraków: Wydawnictwo Literackie, 2011

Janicki, Kamil, *Upadłe damy II Rzeczpospolitej*, Kraków: Wydawnictwo Znak, 2013

Krzywicka, Irena, *Sąd idzie*, Warsaw: Wydawrzystwo Wydawnicze "Rój," 1935

Ibid., *Wyznania gorszycielki*, ed. Agata Tuszyńska, Warsaw: Czytelnik, 2002

Ibid., *Kontrola Współczesności. Wybór międzywojennej publicystyki społecznej i literackiej z lat 1925–1939*, collected and with an introduction by Agata Zawiszewska, Warsaw: Feminoteka, 2008

Kulczycki, Jerzy, *Atakować książką*, Warsaw: Instytut Pamięci Narodowej, 2016

Laniewski, Alfed, *Zbrodnia i łzy. Dwanaście lat pracy prokuratorskiej,* Lwów: Myśl – Wrażenia – Przeżycia, 1936.

Olbrycht, Jan Stanisław, *Medycyna sądowa w procesie karnym*, Warsaw: Państwowy Zakład Wydawnictw Lekarskich, 1957

Ibid., *Wybrane przypadki z praktyki sądowo lekarskiej. Zabójstwo, samobójstwo, czy nieszczęśliwy wypadek?*, Warsaw: Państwowy Zakład Wydawnictw Lekarskich, 1964

Ibid., "Medycyna a kryminalistyka," *Nauka dla Wszystkich*, no. 16, Polska Akademia Nauk – Oddział w Krakowie, 1966

Orłowicz, Mieczysław, *Ilustrowany przewodnik po Lwowie*, Rzeszów: Wydawnictwo Libra PL, 2013

Osiadacz, Maria, *W kręgu zbrodni. Reportaże sądowe*, Warsaw: Wydawnictwo Prawnicze, 1990

Przybyszewska, Stanisława, *Listy. Październik 1929–listopad 1934*, vol. 2, Gdańsk: Wydawnictwo Morskie, 1983

Romański, Marek, *Sprawa Rity Gorgon*, Warsaw: Towarzystwo Wydawnicze "Rój," 1933

Tuszyńska, Agata, *Długie życie gorszycielki. Losy i świat Ireny Krzywickiej*, Warsaw: Iskry, 1987

Widawcki, Jan, *Stulecie krakowskich detektywów*, Warsaw: Wydawnictwo Prawnicze, 1987

Zaremba, Henryk, *Spowiedź ojca zamordowanej Lusi (przyczynek do procesu Gorgonowej)*, Warsaw: Wydawnictwo "Nowa Astrea," 1933

Żurek, Edmund, *Gorgonowa i inni*, Warsaw: Książka i Wiedza, 1973

Files:

State Archive in Kraków: Files of Criminal Case IV 1K 258/32 Margarita Gorgon

Archive of the Jagiellonian University: Jan Olbrycht Archive (DLXXXIV 1–16)

Newspapers:

Express Wieczorny Ilustrowany 1932–1933

Gazeta Lwowska 1932–1933

Ilustrowany Kurier Codzienny 1932–1933

Nowiny Codzienne 1933

Nowy Dziennik 1933

Słowo Polskie 1932

Tajny Detektyw 1932–1934

Selected Articles:

Darecki, Mirosław, "Legenda Gorgonowej," *Kamena* 1977, no. 26, pp. 4–5, http://biblioteka.teatrnn.pl/dlibra/Content/90211/legenda%20gorgonowej.pdf, no access date

Daszczyński, Roman, "Wołali na mnie Gorgonicha," *Duży Format*, wyborcza.pl, goo.gl/EdS7Nc, accessed May 22, 2014

Horoszowski, Paweł, "Od zbrodni do kary," *Biblioteka Problemów*, vol. 69, Warsaw: Państwowe Wydawnictwo Naukowe, 1963

Jakubec, Tomasz, "Mydlarz Tragiczny – czyli historia życia Henryka Zaremby – ojca zamordowanej Lusi," zycieitechnika.blogspot.com, goo.gl/bFtc7q, accessed: November 25, 2014

Kern, Elga, "Prawda o procesie Gorgonowej," *Wiadomości Literackie*, 1932, no. 25

Kocznur, Jan, "Wspomnienie pośmiertne: Jozef Woźniakowski," *Palestra* 1962, no. 6/7

Krzywicka, Irena, "Wielkie manewry sądowe," *Wiadomości Literackie* 1933, no. 23

Ibid., "Wizje i upiory," *Wiadomości Literackie* 1933, no. 24

Ibid., "Dzieje grzechów jej . . . i cudzych," *Wiadomości Literackie* 1933, no. 25

Ibid., "Niepokojący wyrok," *Wiadomości Literackie* 1933, no. 22

Naumowski, Wiesław, "Sprawa Rity Gorgon znów aktualna, *Magazyn Polski* 1957, no. 7

Ostańkowicz, Czesław, "Szukam matki Rity Gorgon," *Magazyn Polski* 1957, no. 11

Przybyszewska, Stanisława, "Rita Gorgon, ofiara zastępcza, *Wiadomości Literackie* 1933, no. 12

Sołtysik, Marek, "Panieńska, Gorgonowa – nieszczęścia i tajemnice," *Palestra* 2009, part 1: nos. 3–4, part 3: nos. 5–6

"Sprawa Gorgonowej. Najgłośniejsze morderstwo ii Rzeczpospolitej," nto.pl, goo.gl/KLHTqn, accessed January 2, 2010

Wiśniacka, Romana, "Zeznania świadków w procesie Gorgonowej w świetle badań naukowych," *Wiadomości Literackie* 1933, no. 20

Włodarski, Łukasz, "Rita Gorgon – morderczyni czy ofiara?," wmrokuhistorii.blogspot.com, goo.gl/L7pmU6, accessed August 11, 2014

Żurek, Edmund, "Sprawa Gorgonowej. Czy nadal zagadka?" *Prawo i Życie* 1973, nos. 3–7

Table of Photographs

CEZARY ŁAZAREWICZ is a Polish journalist who has worked for *Gazeta Wyborcza*, *Przekrój*, and *Polityka*. His books include *Reportaże pomorskie* (Pomeranian Reports, 2012); *Sześć pięter luksusu. Przerwana historia domu braci Jablkowskich* (Six Floors of Luxury: The Interrupted History of the Jablkowski Brothers' House, 2013); *Elegancki morderca* (Elegant Murderer, 2015); *Żeby nie bylo sladów. Sprawa Grzegorza Przemyka* (That There Would Be No Traces: The Case of Grzegorz Przemyk, 2016), for which he received the Nike Literary Prize, the Oscar Halecki Prize, and the MediaTora Prize; and *Tu mówi Polska. Reportaże z Pomorza* (Here is Poland: Reports from Pomerania, 2017). *Żeby nie bylo sladów* was also named Book of the Year by Radio Kraków and was a finalist for the Ryszard Kapuściński Prize.

SEAN GASPER BYE is a translator of Polish fiction, reportage, and drama. He has published translations of *Watercolours* by Lidia Ostalowska, *History of a Disappearance* by Filip Springer, *The King of Warsaw* by Szczepan Twardoch, and *Ellis Island: A People's History* by Malgorzata Szejnert. He's also published shorter pieces in *The Guardian*, *Words Without Borders*, *Catapult*, *World Literature Today*, and elsewhere. He is a winner of the 2016 Asymptote Close Approximations Prize, a 2019 National Endowment for the Arts translation fellow, and former Literature and Humanities Curator at the Polish Cultural Institute New York.